YOUR
SPIRITUAL
GOLD
MIND

The Divine Guide To Financial Freedom

V. John Alexandrov

Fearless Incorporated
Worcester, Massachusetts

Your Spiritual Gold Mind,
The Divine Guide To Financial Freedom
by V. John Alexandrov

Printed in the United States of America.

ISBN 0-9676208-9-9

Library of Congress Catalog Card Number: 99- 096933

First Edition: January 2000

Published by:
Fearless, Incorporated
128 Newton Avenue North
Worcester, MA 01609-1404
1-508-757-0953 phone
1-508-757-0472 fax
1-888-404-6257
Website: www.iamfearless.com
Email: fearless@excelonline.com

Please refer to the back of the book for ordering information regarding this book and other related books and tapes by this author.

To Mary, George,
Alec, Marion & Elizabeth

$\mathcal{T}$ABLE OF CONTENTS

*I*NTRODUCTION

Since publishing *Affirmations Of Wealth-101 Secrets Of Daily Success*, I've had the opportunity to travel throughout the country giving seminars and keynote speeches, as well as speak with thousands of people individually, about their personal challenges and successes in life. This has been, and continues to be, my mission and purpose in life—helping others to succeed and fully utilize their God given talents.

The more I listened to the common challenges we each face, the more I realized there is a common thread, a missing link, between professing our desire to be wealthy or successful, and actually attaining it. In other words, most people truly want to succeed and are willing to dedicate themselves to being and doing so, yet there is a dark mental cloud that continually drifts over us, preventing the rays of success from manifesting in our lives. So many people have told me, "they wish their prayers would be answered," or "they are doing all the right things," yet success seems as elusive as a mirage in the middle of the desert. I finally, after months of contemplating this issue, developed a new paradigm, a new way of looking at this challenge, the result of which is embodied in this book, **Your Spiritual Gold Mind.** After countless interviews and personal coaching sessions, I was enlightened to the following truths:

1. Most people want to succeed, they just don't know how to accept success.

2. Most people never become wealthy because they lack a truthful understanding of the relationship between God, themselves and money.

3. Most people associate success with money yet have a poor relationship with money and what it actually represents.

4. All of us have a money heritage which either enhances or limits our ability to create, generate or accept wealth.

5. Having wealth and money (and maintaining and proliferating each one) is directly related to our inner spiritual economy.

6. Anyone can become successful and wealthy, spiritually and financially, after acknowledging and accepting the goodness of money. We can regenerate our ability to create wealth by following certain spiritual and money principles.

7. We each have a spiritual and financial *gold mind* within, which continually delivers to us exactly what we profess spiritually, verbally, mentally and physically. Our spiritual and financial *gold mind* mirrors our faith.

8. Our spiritual *gold mind* is waiting for each of us to tap into it for God's sake and for ours.

9. There is a manifestation process (a proven method) to claim, attain and accept wealth, spiritually and financially, that always works if we choose to have faith.

I must declare up front that this is not a "religious" book or a "religious" philosophy, nor does it contain a "religious" agenda. **Your Spiritual Gold Mind** is a book about *intentioned enlightenment and the manifestation and acceptance of wealth, including money, through spiritual means.* Nor is this book a "contemporary" thesis by a "contemporary" thinker about the development of prosperity. *This is purely and simply a book which reveals the truth about wealth, and the spiritual and financial laws about wealth, money and prosperity, which have been utilized by millions of people for thousands of years.* There have been so many "new age" prospectives bantered about in recent years that one begins to wonder, "what is the truth?" We read and hear things such as, "there is no right or wrong, only bi-polar experiences," or " our souls are experiencing what they must experience right now because in past lives we didn't experience these things." There are hundreds more new age doctrines such as, "we must disassociate ourselves from money and material things in order to find true prosperity." I have finally concluded, after interviewing thousands of people, that most of these new age doctrines are convenient excuses not to accept responsibility for our own personal choices.

Your Spiritual Gold Mind *explains the truth about spiritual principles, the power of God, and the manifestation of all the good that is ours by birthright.* Please keep an important fact in mind while reading this book: there is power in simplicity. The principles you will be reading and implementing have been used for thousands of years. They were used by Moses, Jesus, Mother Teresa, as well as many of the great entrepreneurs of the world. They are used daily to manifest dreams and goals of all types, and to glorify God for His love and greatness. These principles are used to create wealth of all types, and yes, to develop financial fortunes and material things. Contrary to the theories you may have read or heard elsewhere, in this book you will learn money is good; in fact, money is God in action. You will learn not to disassociate yourself from the real world, but how to use your divines to embrace and accept the abundance of the real world; as well as how to use it for the good of God, yourself and many other people.

We live in an ever changing world which tries to persuade us to forget about principles and focus on new prospectives. I will admit, learning and implementing new prospectives can be invigorating and financially profitable. However, forgetting about spiritual principles, and how they apply to our individual and collective lives, is a sure path to destruction (history has proven this many times).

As you are reading this book, you may find some similarities to other practitioners of the *gold mind* principles: Jesus, many of the prophets, Florence Scovel Shinn, Dr. Joseph Murphy, Eric Butterworth, Shakti Gawain, Frederic Lehrman and John Randolph Price to name a few. I highly recommend you study their lives, read their works, and implement their doctrines as well, but try to do so in a modern day context. **Your Spiritual Gold Mind** takes the principles of love, prosperity, abundance, gratitude, truth, vision, faith, the spoken word, choice acceptance, wealth (and several others) and relates them to the realities of today's world. In the past, taxes, credit cards, electronic banking, e-commerce, and the Internet were not discussed in spiritual terms, nor were they taken into consideration when explaining the development and acceptance of money and financial wealth through spiritual principles. Today, however, all these things are a reality of life which we must understand in real and spiritual terms in order to establish and accept spiritual and financial freedom.

As you read this book, you will see scripture references at the conclusion of each affirmation. These have been included for those of you who enjoy, and include, Bible study as part of your daily life. I am not a theologian, nor do I have any theological training. The scripture references were collected be me during years of reading and study. At first glance, many of them may not seem to have a direct relationship to the affirmation you are reading; but if you do some research, you will find they are all related to this philosophy. Since the references were collected over a long period of time, you will see they have come from different Bible versions and may not exactly correspond to your Bible. For those of you who do not study or use the Bible, these scripture references are not necessary or crucial to the understanding and use of this book or the manifestation process. You may simply read them or not, but it will not diminish your understanding or the usefulness of this book if you do not read them.

It is my goal to help the countless people who are always striving and searching for success and wealth, to achieve (or maybe more importantly, to accept) them, whatever they represent for you. When you are reading and using **Your Spiritual Gold Mind,** please keep in mind the following:

1. Developing and accepting financial wealth is not a secret, *it is a process.*

2. We typically get from life what *we prepare for,* spiritually and financially.

3. We are all perfect expression's of *God's love.*

4. We live in a world of *divine grace* (a world of perfect abundance), not in a karmic world of give and take (limited abundance).

We all have been given almost unbelievable power from God; the ability to be love, give love, and receive love. We have been given the ability to dream, to act, and most importantly, to choose and accept (we can tap into the world of divine grace any time we want to). When we accept the truth about ourselves, accept the grace of God, and act in accordance with the divine plan of our lives, we can be, do and have all things. When we accept God, we can accept anything. When we work with God, we can work for anything. When we have God, we have everything.

How To Use This Book

The format of **Your Spiritual Gold Mind** is probably unlike any other book you have read or used. If you read *Affirmations Of Wealth – 101 Secrets Of Daily Success,* you are somewhat familiar with the process of reading with intention, self-discovery and journal writing. In **Your Spiritual Gold Mind,** the process of manifesting dreams and goals has been elevated to a new level. You will journey through a self-discovery process, read new insights (and discover new insights) about God, yourself and money, and you will put your thoughts into action through various spiritual and financial exercises.

I recommend you read through the entire book once before taking notes or completing the exercises. After you have read through the entire book, turn to the *Spiritual And Financial Self-Discovery Checklist* and complete the exercises that are appropriate for you. Then begin reading through the affirmations again. Some of them will "click" or "strike at your heart or soul." Take note of these affirmations and complete any recommended exercises. Also, after reading each affirmation, take notes in the "Thoughts" section reserved after each affirmation. Then write some short goals or priorities to complete in the "Actions" section. This will create a wonderful journal, treasure map and foundation for the realization of your dreams and goals.

There is no right or wrong way to use this book. Some people read one affirmation a day, some more. Some people use specific affirmations as a guide to develop their own affirmations: this is great. I recommend you do the same as well. Read, and more importantly, USE this book. Do so at your own pace, in your own way. Personalize your book as much as possible. Write in it often and pay special attention to the notes. ***Most importantly, however, you must put your thoughts and what you learn into action.*** Have fun. Share your new insights with others. Create and share your wealth for God's sake and for yours.

The Meaning Of Words

Throughout this book, you will see several familiar terms which may have different meanings in the context of this writing than in every day use. Keep in mind when reading and using the principles in **Your Spiritual Gold Mind,** the power of the spoken and written word is extraordinary. The definitions of the following terms, and your use and understanding of them, will help you focus in, and fully utilize, the power of your *gold mind.*

God:

As mentioned in the introduction to this book, this is not a "religious" philosophy; it is a spiritual philosophy. I have no desire to evoke a certain religion or religious philosophy as part of this process. We all have a spirituality about us, a spirit within us. There is no denying there is a God, a Creator or Infinite Intelligence in this universe that is far superior to us. We were created by God to live, prosper and proliferate abundance and His goodness every day. My personal belief is that God is the Holy Trinity, represented by the Father, Son and the Holy Spirit. I refer to God as "He" and "Him" because my Savior, Jesus Christ, continually refers to God as "My Father." Your beliefs may be different. *The basic nature of this book and the fundamental spiritual and financial principles herein are temporal; they apply to people of all religions, all faiths and to anyone who is secular in thinking as well.* If you want or need to substitute the word God with the words "Higher Power" or "Creator" or something similar, do so. But make sure you stay true to the processes revealed in this book.

Wealth:

Fundamental to the understanding of this philosophy is that wealth and money are very separate and distinct things. Wealth is much more than money, cars or lavish homes. There are many people who obtain many material possessions but never become wealthy because they lack a basic understanding of truth, spirituality and personal responsibility in their lives. Wealth is a balance of spiritual fulfillment and devotion as well as love, physical and mental health, family happiness, true friendships, social kindness—as well as money. Now don't deceive yourself into financial poverty or mediocrity because you think money isn't important.

Money is as important as all other forms of wealth. It is my goal to help you create, attract and circulate all types of wealth in your life, including money.

Prosperity:

Many people confuse the words "prosperity" and "abundance." You will see me use both words several times in this book, many times in the same affirmation. Prosperity means success or financial well being. The term prosperity carries with it a feeling of progressiveness. Prosperity relates financial and personal success with action; developing and maintaining a thriving life spiritually, physically and financially. But in its most basic form, prosperity means financial or economic success.

Abundance:

To be abundant, or to have abundance, means to have plenty, have more than enough, or to be bountiful. This is not an economic or financial term, although we can enjoy financial abundance. Abundance is a natural state of being; it requires no effort, only an understanding, consciousness and dedication to living in an abundant state of mind. Remember that our physical realities are a true reflection of our inner realities. Living an abundant life spiritually and mentally leads to an abundant life physically and financially.

Riches:

Again, although many people perceive the term "rich" to be a financial state, the truest definition of the word rich means to be fruitful or fertile. In other words, people who are rich are full of ideas and actions which, when cultivated, produce remarkable returns. These returns may be spiritual, financial or both. People who are rich continuously harvest and replenish themselves and others with love, spirit, thoughts, actions and money.

Money:

Money, in a very real sense, is something accepted or given as a medium of exchange. Money can be represented by many things, but for most people it is represented by cash (dollar bills, coins, etc.). Money can also be abstract. For example, promissory notes, certificates of deposit and stock certificates represent money, but not in the form of cash. As we earn or attract more money, we typically convert it from the real form (cash), into money in the abstract (certificates of deposit, etc.). Money, as described in this book, is also a form of energy with incredible properties, just like many other forms of energy. We pass on our individual energy (our thoughts, dreams, love, hate, envy, etc.) when we use or invest our money. Our money is the physical representation of our thoughts and beliefs which carries forth a part of us everywhere it goes.

Manifestation:

The term manifestation means to develop into physical reality. I continually use the words manifest and manifestation in this book and the related exercises. You will read about (and hopefully use) a "manifestation process" which will help you convert your spiritual and mental energy into physical reality. So manifestation is a process of converting thoughts into physical reality.

Faith:

An entire book could be written about this one word. As described here, the term faith means belief coupled with action; the ability to take action on your dreams and goals and to follow the divine plan of your life, even though you may not see any physical evidence of their manifestation. Faith also describes your commitment to God's plan for your life, trusting that this is the right plan for you (and for Him), and carrying out your divine plan to completeness. Remember that faith without action is dead (it is no faith at all). Belief and trust in God, and the unseen, while maintaining your faith as evidenced by your actions; this is true faith.

Spiritual/Spirituality:

You will see the term spiritual throughout the upcoming pages. For a word that seems so obvious, it is very difficult to describe what spirituality really is. I think the best way to describe someone who is spiritual is to characterize them as godlike. Spiritual people have many godlike attributes. They are blessed in thought and action, boundless in their love, virtuous and pure in their intentions, yet they are all powerful. You will see me refer to the "spiritual economy" several times. And the very title of this book, **Your Spiritual Gold Mind,** portrays our ability to live abundant, prosperous and faithful lives through spiritual thoughts and actions (by becoming one with God in conscious intention and through our actions). Look again at the key words in the definition of the word *spiritual*; godlike, blessed, divine, boundless, virtuous, all powerful, pure, eternal, devout. These words not only depict the concept of spirituality, they set forth our goal; to be spiritual in all that we are and all that we do. This is true spirituality.

Truth:

When we are truthful with ourselves, we exhibit and confirm our integrity, genuineness, authenticity and fidelity. Truth is a principle, similar to love; it is eternal, unlimited in scope and application, as well as necessary for spiritual awakening and development. Think about these examples for a moment:

1. When we are true to God and His divine plan for our lives, we confirm our very reason for being. We are authentic, honest and humble.

2. When we are true to ourselves, we are genuine in thought and action and we exhibit fidelity to our very being through faith.

3. When we are true to our calling, we confirm our belief and faith in God and to our personal integrity.

4. When we do all things with truth, we develop freedom through spirituality and principle centered living. There is a quote inscribed on the face of the courthouse in my hometown. It reads " Obedience To Law Is Liberty." The same holds true for our dedication to living a spiritual and truthful life; when we are obedient and surrender to God, His plan, His love, and truly think and act spiritually, we are liberated.

Investment:

When we "invest" something or "invest in" something, we are taking an empowering action. You will soon learn, when we invest in something our mentality and the very essence of who we are travels with our investment. We actually infuse ourselves into the company, person or relationship we invest in. Be very careful when investing love, time and energy (including your money), because your results typically will reflect your mentality at the time you invest. Always be spiritual in your thinking and in your actions when investing anything—then you will see marvelous returns.

Grace:

We live in a world of grace; a world of love, thanksgiving, beauty and perfect abundance. This is the natural world God created and established for us; not a world of give and take, lack or limitation. The only lack or limitation we ever experience is created by us, through our thoughts, actions (or inaction) and lack of faith. Perfect abundance is all around us and in us; it is right before our eyes. All we have to do is attune ourselves to it by loving God, devoting to His plan for our lives, and accepting the flow of wealth that is ours by birthright. Grace and abundance are the natural way.

Divine/Divines:

I have already referred to the "divine plan" several times in this book and you will see it many more times. We each have a purpose, as well as many unique God given talents. Our divine self is the self God intended us to be. We each have godlike qualities and an all-knowing intuition. We each have a truth that was established just for us. When we find our truth (or surrender to it), use our godlike qualities, and do so to carry out God's intended purpose for us, we are divine.

Success:

One of the greatest definitions of success I have ever seen/heard was described by Napoleon Hill as, "having anything you want in life without violating the laws of God or the rights of other people." I would alter this slightly and describe success as *being, manifesting, having or accepting anything you want in life without violating the laws of God, without violating your individual truth (devoting yourself to God's divine plan for you), and without violating the rights of other people.*

Financial Freedom:

Financial freedom is a state of consciousness in which you can be, do or have anything—regardless of the amount of money you have.

The Spiritual Economy

The spiritual economy is a state of consciousness. In the truest sense, spiritual economies are created when we discover, attune ourselves with, and surrender to God's divine plan for our lives. When this happens, we become a consciousness with and for God and we open the channels for amazing flows of abundance and prosperity. Our individual spiritual economies thrive and regenerate on love, gratitude, faith, acceptance, divine devotion and truth. It seems strange doesn't it; describing the economy in terms of truth and love instead of gross national product or interest rates? But the key to our individual prosperity and to the collective long term wealth of any nation, is consciousness. As we individually and collectively move closer to, and establish ourselves in the consciousness of God, we prosper in all aspects of our lives. Lasting financial wealth requires a spiritual commitment, spiritual investments and spiritual accountability; the willingness to give and receive love, wealth and God's direction and goodness in every aspect of our lives.

As a result of creating and proliferating our individual spiritual economies, we learn not only how to create a life of spiritual well being, but also how to open the channels for the manifestation of material wealth and money. Keep in mind, continuously, that money is good-money is God in action. However, our focus must always be on God first, and the good we can create for Him as a result of our dedication to His plan, with His love. *If we begin to idolize money or material things, we shall have sinned and we shall be broke. The manifestation of money must come as a result of who we are, and the love, time and energy we give or invest in the truth.*

Therefore, it should be our goal to glorify God in our thoughts and actions; to become one with the Divine Mind, the consciousness of God. Our spirit, our very thoughts and our very soul always travel with our energy, including our money. To create and manifest wealth, we must give wealth. To create and manifest love, we must give love. To create and manifest abundance, we must be abundant. This is the only true way to manifest wealth and continuously replenish the universe and ourselves with prosperity.

Our Money Heritage

For many of you, this is the moment you have been waiting for; now we are going to start talking about money. Just as we each have a genetic heritage, we each have a money heritage as well. With near certainty, we take on the characteristics of our family's money genealogy. Think back to the way your parents or other close family members handled their financial affairs, then take a good hard look at your financial situation right now. How many similarities are there? It is astonishing, isn't it? Think about the spending, savings and debt patterns of your parents. Are yours similar? More importantly, think back to some initial impressions or thoughts your parents instilled in you about money or financial affairs. What were they, and how have they affected your life? If you are really honest, you will agree they have had a dramatic impact on your life.

As you read the *Affirmations For Spiritual And Financial Enrichment,* you will notice several affirmations on this subject. Why? Because what we consciously and unconsciously learned and absorbed from our parents has a tendency to stay with us forever. If your parents tended to "play it safe," you will have a strong tendency to do the same. If your parents were "gamblers," always taking risks, you most likely will do so as well. If your parents were always in debt, buying things on credit, or felt guilty about money, that may also be your perceived fate. If your parents were responsible with their money, invested it wisely and manifested wealth truthfully, most likely you will as well. A typical pattern I often see is people striving and working hard to be successful, but financial emergencies and losses continue to manifest in their lives. This is primarily due to a deep seeded family heritage of lack, limitation, guilt, jealousy or emotional deceit.

We each have a defining moment, or series of defining moments, in our financial lives. These defining moments typically occurred when we were young. We may have lost some money and were chastised for it publicly. We may have been told that people with money are "bad." We may have been told we must work hard for our money, resulting in a "work hard" heritage instead of a "creating wealth and prosperity" heritage. I could go on and on, but a crucial exercise for you to do right now is to take out a pen and a piece of paper, and write down the most vivid experiences you had with money as a child. What do you remember about money? Why do you remember this? Were your first money experiences pleasurable or painful? Why? When you manifest wealth and receive money, do you feel guilty or ashamed about it? Why? Do you have a hard time accepting money or gifts? Why? If you become successful, do you feel as if you will betray your family heritage? Why? Continue on and write down all your feelings about money, what your current financial situation is, and why you believe you created the financial condition (good or bad) you are in right now. This may be a painful exercise for you, but doing so will bring into your consciousness all of your feelings, emotions, fears and beliefs about money. *And remember, consciousness is one of the keys to financial freedom.*

Self-Worth vs. Net Worth

Our self-worth should never be determined by our net worth. Take a look at the definition of financial freedom again: financial freedom is a state of consciousness in which you can be, do or have anything regardless of the amount of money you have. In other words, you can remain true to yourself and your calling regardless of whether you have a few dollars or millions of dollars. We are directed, and we are obligated to each live a rich and fulfilling life whether we have money or not. *A few words of caution here. This book is going to help you manifest anything you want in life, including money, but do not allow the size of your bank account to determine the quality of your life. Be true to God's principles, continually enrich yourself and others, and you will be wealthy-personally and financially.*

Our self-worth should never be determined by our net worth, but our net worth may be, and most often is, determined by our self-worth. In other words, in order to be financially wealthy, you must believe you are worthy of it. The main reason most people do not achieve financial wealth and freedom is because of fear, low self-esteem, a poor money heritage and/or emotional heritage, or because they have an addiction (addictions are many times the result of your emotional heritage, fear or low self-esteem). Let's take a look at each of these challenges to personal and financial freedom to see how they affect our financial lives and our personal spiritual economy.

Fear

The only two natural fears we have are the fear of falling and the fear of loud noises. Where did the rest come from? We inherit fears through watching and listening to other people, by watching television, and from absorbing other unwarranted and fearful information. If we are a fearful person, we are most likely fearful financially as well. Many people have specific money fears which inhibit them their entire lives, and which create a fearful money heritage for generations. What are your fears about money? How did these develop in your life? Why do you have these fears?

Keep in mind an important fact; money is innocent. Money cannot perpetuate fears, solve problems or create wealth. Only people can do these things. If you are a fearful person and you create more financial wealth, you will be more fearful with (an maybe of) your money. If you are a fearless person, you will continue to be fearless with your money. So, an important step in developing financial freedom is eliminating (or at least properly managing) fear. If you live in fear, no matter how much money you have, you can never be financially free. In the *Affirmations For Spiritual And Financial Enrichment,* there are several affirmations that will help you with this. Use these affirmations often. They will help you to clear the channel for the manifestation of your desires.

Erasing The Old Myths About Money

There are several myths about money which must be addressed, understood and eliminated before manifesting financial wealth. The first is the age old lie... money is the root of all evil. Many people live their entire lives innocently perpetuating this lie. They claim since this quote has a Biblical foundation and is embodied in scripture, this must be true. If you do your homework, you will find this reference is neither Biblical or anywhere in scripture. If you read the Gospel according to John, you will see he said, "The love of money is the root of all evil." In other words, we cannot idolize money. Idolatry is a sure path to self destruction. Money, by itself, cannot create evil or do evil things. Only people can create or do evil things. *Money is good, money is innocent, money is pure; it is only our intentions that can destroy the goodness of money.*

The next myth we often hear is that in the Book Of Revelation, Jesus said, "A camel would fit through the eye of a needle before a rich man would enter the kingdom of heaven." Go back and look at the definition of the term "rich." Rich is not a financial term, it is a description of a state of consciousness or a state of mind. Jesus was referring to people who are rich in conceit, selfishness and self-aggrandizement. He wasn't referring to people who were financially well-off. *In order to enter the kingdom of heaven, which by the way lies within you and is all around you, you must be rich in love, thought and action.*

Another myth which devastates many people is the concept that they must "suffer" or "sacrifice greatly" now in order to enter the Promised Land or in order to display religious piety. Discipline certainly is a key to spiritual and financial freedom, suffering is not. *The spiritual economy, living in a world of grace and perfect abundance, living as an expression of God's love, requires no sacrifice.* What they require is love, the glorification of God through prosperous and abundant thoughts and actions, and constant gratitude and replenishment. Forget about suffering and sacrifice and focus on how you are going to glorify God through your thoughts, action and love.

The final myth we will address here (there are others addressed in the affirmations) is the myth that hard work leads to financial freedom. Quite honestly, I have seen hard work ruin many lives and devastate the money heritage of many families. If you are true to your calling, glorify God through your thoughts, actions and chosen profession...and you love what you do, how can this be hard work? Many people work so hard to "make a living," they have no room for abundance and prosperity. They are so focused on surviving, they have no time or energy to live. Many people use "hard work" as an excuse or justification for mediocrity or financial indifference. They say, "after all, I am working so hard, I don't have the time or energy to do what I really want to do." Although hard work certainly can be a noble attribute, it has almost no bearing on the manifestation of financial wealth. If you view what you do as hard work, you should seriously consider changing professions. *You must love what you do and do what you love; this is the path to spiritual and financial freedom.*

Eliminate these myths from your thinking. Replenish yourself, spiritually and financially, with thoughts of abundance, love and the glorification of God. From here you can manifest everything which is yours by divine right.

MANIFESTING WEALTH

ℳANIFESTING WEALTH

The Manifestation Process

In the introduction, I declared that developing wealth is not a secret—it is a process. The manifestation process is about to be revealed to you. In order to establish the proper mindset to use this process however, **you must understand that you deserve to be wealthy, it is your birthright to be wealthy and everything you could ever dream of, desire or hope for, is already within your grasp.** Each of us is already ripe with the harvest; all we must do now is allow it to manifest, to become reality. You already have, or have to the ability to obtain, everything you need to manifest your wealth. It is right before your eyes and within your reach. This process is going to "bring into consciousness" the opportunities, the vehicles for achievement, and the directions for manifesting anything you want from life. This is called mining the gold from within, and it is a gift from God.

Mining The Gold From Within

Step 1: Pray.

Let's explore the concept of prayer for a moment. Prayer is the primary method by which we stay attuned to God, receive His revelations, stay centered in God's consciousness, prepare to carry forth the divine plan for our lives, and give gratitude. Wow! Do we really accomplish all of this when we pray? Yes...and a lot more. I am often asked the question, "How should I pray?" or "Is there a specific method of prayer I should use?" It is my personal opinion that there is no "right" or "wrong" way to pray. Some key points, however, are to stay attuned to God, be specific in your appeals, give thanks for all that you have and what you are about to receive (whether these are intangible items such as love, courage, faith, or tangible items such as money or material things). The most effective method of prayer for me is to carry on a continual conversation with God. I literally talk with God continuously. My wife and children are always asking me, "Did you just say something?" This is usually because I am praying with a running conversation, or I am affirming my intentions or beliefs.

The different components of prayer set forth above are certainly not a comprehensive or mandatory format for prayer, but it may be helpful for you to understand each one.

Staying attuned to God. God is everywhere, God is everything. Staying attuned to God means *we seek out and receive God* in many things. Sometimes when we feel alone or out of touch with God, it isn't because God has abandoned us, has better things to do, or is testing us. It is because we fail to see and hear God in the obvious and simple things in life. Look around you now. What do you see? Is there a reflection of God somewhere there? What is it? Who is it? If you feel like you are losing touch with God, stop for a moment and seek Him out in the obvious. Make God a part of your life, in everything you do.

Be specific in your appeals...don't be afraid to ask! If you take nothing else away from this entire book except this one point, I will have succeeded in helping you carry out your mission in life. *You must ask God for what you want and be truly willing to carry it out and/or accept it.* So many people feel they can't ask God for what they want because it may be a sign of selfishness or weakness. If you can't ask your Creator, who can you ask? *Asking is a sign of humility, reverence and respect. When you appeal to God in prayer, you are acknowledging His greatness and you display your faith in Him.* Show your respect and humility by asking, do so with pure intent and an honest heart, and you shall receive. Seek, knock and ask!

Receive God's revelations. As important to carrying on a continual conversation with God, and staying attuned to His goodness, is listening. Aren't our minds amazing? We truly each possess a spiritual *gold mind.* We seek answers and God always reveals Himself, or the answer to our prayers, either through subconscious messages, direct revelations or physical suggestion. It is our job to hear and see the answers, accept them, and put them into action when required. You know you always receive the answers to your prayers. Your answers may not come how and when you demand them however. In most cases they come when you can comprehend and accept them, and are willing to put them to use. Stop trying to humanize them, to adapt them to your paradigms. Accept the answers to your prayers and take action.

Stay centered in God's consciousness. God is omnipotent, ever present, always there, always loving. We must continually center ourselves in God's love, presence and all-knowing intelligence. When we begin to go astray and disassociate ourselves from God, and the humility of being a part of His consciousness, we lose touch with love, His presence, and we lose our strength and faith. Always keep God in mind and continually accept His presence.

Pray for others. If you really want to experience the opening of the flood gates spiritually and financially, try praying for other people. Be specific in your personal appeals to God, but also seek out goodness for others. Pray genuinely for others and truly seek out God's intercession on their behalf. You will be amazed at what will happen for them and for you.

Continually give thanks. In order to be truly spiritual, to manifest our dreams and intentions, we must have gratitude in our hearts and minds. Thanksgiving does not come once a year, it is a 24-hour a day commitment. God is all-knowing... He knows your true intentions. He accepts genuine gratitude as your intention to proliferate His plan. Don't give false gratitude as a means to an end. Be truly grateful for all the love you have, all the God-given gifts you have received, and for the manifestation of your dreams, because you already have them within your midst.

Commit time to prayer every day. It is both a sign of respect and love for God, as well as a means of preparation. Through prayer we can prepare for and accept the goodness of God in all forms. Live your life as a prayer and you will know God. Live your life as a prayer and you will undoubtedly carry out the divine plan for your life....you will be immersed in wealth for all of your days.

Step 2: Start dreaming again.

In order to manifest anything, you must be able to see it, believe in it, and have it within your grasp—spiritually and mentally. Dreaming allows you to regenerate your enthusiasm and gives you the strength to carry out your goals with a sense of purpose. There are many scripture references describing our ability to attain our desires through proper vision. But in order to establish a vision, a clear mental picture of what we desire to manifest (of what we want to be, do or have), we must re-establish our dreams. What have you always wanted to be, do or have? If you had all the money you ever desired, what would you be or do? These questions will lead you in the right direction. At this point you must stop reading, go and find a notebook or a piece of paper, and write down your dreams and aspirations. Give yourself a 5-minute time limit and write down as many dreams and goals as you can. This may be a difficult exercise for you because many of us have forgotten how to dream. Do it anyway and do it now (I'm serious. Stop reading and do this exercise now!). Welcome back. You have just taken a very important step in the manifestation of your dreams. First, you have made a mental commitment to accomplishing them because they are in writing. Second, you now can picture your compelling reasons for making the changes you may need to make to accomplish your goals. And third, you have established the foundation of a prayer list for making your specific appeals known to God. Congratulations!!! You are well on your way to living your dreams.

Step 3: Write your goals.

After your dreams are "before your eyes" (they are actually on paper in front of you), you must then write them as goals. For those of you who are not experienced at goal writing, start by writing one goal only and focus on that. When that goal is accomplished, go to your next goal and do the same. For those of you who are experienced goal writers, write as many goals as you feel are appropriate for you. One word of caution, however; having too many goals is like having no goals at all. If you have too many goals you are trying to manifest at one time, you will lose your focus. So be disciplined and prioritize your goals. Only work on the goals which are the most important to you right now.

When you write down your goals, you should write a short description of what you want to accomplish, why you want to accomplish it, the means or method you will use to accomplish your goal, the date by which you will accomplish it, and a clear picture of what you will do with the results or fruit of your goal. Here is a simple format to follow:

My goal is:

I want to accomplish this goal because:

I will accomplish this goal by taking the following actions by the following dates:

Action To Be Taken _____ **Expected Completion Date** _____

My goal will be 100% accomplished by: _____
                                                                                    (Date)

Upon accomplishing my goal, I (and/or others) will experience the following emotions:

Upon accomplishing my goal, I (and/or others) will benefit in the following manner:

Upon accomplishing my goal, I specifically will buy, have, be or do the following:

Go back to your dream list, take your most important dream and convert it to a written goal using the suggested format. If applicable, go to your next dream and write it as a goal, and so on. Review your goals periodically, weekly or monthly, but do it consistently.

I am often asked, "Why is writing my goals necessary, I already know what they are?" As you may have read in *Affirmations Of Wealth – 101 Secrets of Daily Success,* the act of writing your goals is crucial to the manifestation process. When you write a goal, you stake your claim to it. There are countless references in the Bible, and other spiritual writings, to "staking our claim" to what we desire from life. Writing our goals establishes our claim to them, allows us to take ownership of them now, clearly describes what we desire, and sets out a clear road map on how to accomplish them. Writing our goals also holds us accountable to accomplishing them...in essence, we create a contract with God and ourselves for the attainment of our goals. We, literally, inscribe them upon our minds when we inscribe them on paper. If we remain principle centered, fully utilize our God given talents, remain faithful (and if necessary, patient), our goals will be accomplished.

Step 4: Synchronization.

Now that we have written our goals, we must synchronize ourselves with the truth. In other words, what is the truth about myself and how am I going to accomplish my goals truthfully. If you have an addiction, whatever it may be, most of your goals will be very difficult to accomplish until you address, confront and take control over your addiction (take control over yourself). Addictions rob us of time, money, energy, love, consciousness and truth. No matter how inconsequential you think your addiction is, it will continually control you or you will lose control to it, thereby keeping you from being truthful to yourself and to God.

So how do we synchronize ourselves to and with the truth? We all know what our truth's are in life—you wrote them down on your dream list. Your dream list has revealed the truth about who and what you want to be. Now you must exercise the love and courage it takes to be and do them. Here is an exercise that will help you with this:

Take out a piece of paper and draw a line down the middle. In the left column write down everything you love to do...everything! Don't hold back here. You may love to read, take walks, teach, drive in the country, play golf, etc. Whatever you love to do, write it down on the left side of the page. On the right side of the page, write down a (or several) career, profession, service, entrepreneurial opportunity or hobby you can create or procure using the substance of what you love to do. Keep in mind, when you do what you love to do, you are probably very good at it, or at a minimum, you are passionate enough about it to dedicate the necessary energy to be good at it. Also, when you do what you love, you clear your mind (clear the channels) for wonderful and wondrous messages from God. Your intuition will be abound with His glory. All you have to do is carry it out.

Now some of you are already thinking things like, "I'd love to be a mountain guide but I need to support my family...I can't really afford to do what I really want to do." Where is your faith? The truth has been revealed to you. You don't have to drop everything and run to your new profession. Make a transition plan. Exercise some discipline. For example, it took me almost three years to transition from practicing law to writing, speaking and dedicating to my network marketing career, full time. You can do it as well.

Synchronize yourself with the truth. Discover the truth in what you love. This is God's mandate for you. Accept His gift. Accept His love. Accept your wealth.

Step 5-a: Visualize and affirm every day.

Using the technique of visualization allows us to have a clear mental picture of our dreams and goals. Visualization allows us to immerse ourselves in greatness while taking ownership and seeing now what is manifesting in our lives. Like affirmations, visualizing must be as natural as possible. If you force a picture into your mind which causes doubt, confusion, or just doesn't feel right to you, your visualization can do more harm than good. The most effective method of visualization is to ask God to deliver the proper mental images or pictures to you for the manifestation of your dreams. For example, if you want to visualize a new home, ask God to deliver to you the "right picture" of the "right house," the one that is yours by divine right. Also, ask God for a clear picture of what to do with the fruits of your accomplishments. In other words, ask Him for guidance as to what you should do with your new home, new found money or the love you will receive through Him. You will be simply amazed at what happens. Here is an exercise for you. For the next week, prior to going to sleep, quietly pray or affirm, "God, thank you for giving me the perfect pictures for the manifestation of my dreams and goals." You will quickly begin to see things differently. Your perception will change. You may have dreams that seem extraordinary. People, places and things will begin to appear that you never noticed before. Take note of these images (or realities). This is God delivering your answers, either in the abstract or in reality. Write them down and hold them in your mind. Affix yourself to them and they will affix themselves to you.

Continually hold these pictures in your mind, then "upgrade" your visualizations by adding emotion to them. In other words, don't just see your dreams and goals—feel, taste, smell, hear and touch them as well. This is a very effective technique. Here is a quick exercise that will demonstrate the power of emotion and how reality can manifest. Close your eyes for a moment and think of a fresh lemon. Picture it clearly in your mind. Run your hands over it. What does it feel like? Hold it up to your nose and smell it. How does it smell? Is it bright yellow or a shade of yellow? Take out a knife and cut it in half. Watch the fresh juice spray out of the lemon, then smell it. What an aroma. Now put it up to your lips and taste it. Fresh lemon juice. Is it bitter or sweet, warm or cold? How does it taste? Is your mouth watering yet?

Do you get the point? For the past few moments, that lemon was real. You saw it, smelled it, felt it and tasted it. You could hear the sound of the knife cutting though it. For a few moments, you owned that lemon in every way possible (a few of you may actually have one appear out of nowhere in the next few hours or days). *The same holds true for all of our dreams and goals. We already can and do own them. We can live in a visual kingdom of wealth. Our subconscious gold mind's are just waiting to be mined. Keep digging, affixing your thoughts and visions to your mental images, and sooner or later, if you remain faithful, your*

dreams will manifest before your eyes. Totally immerse yourself in your dreams and goals. Live in them as if they are real...because they are!

Step 5-b: Affirmations.

For a full discourse on the necessity and power of affirmations, you may want to read or review *Affirmations Of Wealth – 101 Secrets Of Daily Success.* In their truest form, affirmations are statements of belief. Along with prayer and visualization, affirmations clear the channel for the manifestation of your dreams and goals. Through affirmation we can eliminate or manage fear, develop courage and faith, declare our worthiness, and establish the foundation of all forms of success. Also, our prayers, affirmations and visualizations tend to "magnetize" us. They establish us as the foundation to which all things can be attracted. Now be aware, affirmations and prayer can be counter productive if used in a negative frame of mind. If we pray and affirm with a lack mind or with limited thoughts, we will have great difficulty in manifesting our dreams. We must have faith, belief and positive expectations. At the bare minimum, we must be open to the concept that affirmations "might" work for us. However, the stronger your belief and expectations, the more faith you have, the better the results will be.

The power of words (whether written, spoken or delivered through our thoughts) and the results they produce, are irrefutable. The power of the tongue is more powerful than any weapon. Words and thoughts are two of our greatest gifts and can be either our great allies or great enemies. The Bible, and other spiritual writings, are full of parables and examples of the power of the spoken and written word. You certainly can, and continuously do, *declare a thing and it is done.*

In order for an affirmation to be the most effective, it should either be self-written or acceptable to your mind. If you read an affirmation and immediately get a negative or uncertain reaction, don't try to force it into your subconscious (by the way this strong negative reaction may be a sign that you need to work on this area of your life). Develop an affirmation(s) that flows for you or is natural for you. I have provided 101 affirmations as samples for you in the *Affirmations For Spiritual And Financial Enrichment* section of this book. If any of the affirmations "feel right" to you, use them; if not, write your own. Also, if you are not experienced in using affirmations or have a difficult time accepting them, you may want to begin by using "one word" affirmations.

Simply repeat to yourself: "wealth," "prosperity," "love," "gratitude," or any other word(s) which helps you focus on the mindset necessary to manifest your dreams and desires. Here are some guidelines to follow when writing and using affirmations.

1. Be conscious of the words you use. Remember, what we profess we eventually possess.

2. Write your affirmations in the present tense.

3. Use the words, "I Am" as much as possible in your affirmations.

4. Repeat your affirmations verbally, and in writing, for a period of 30 consecutive days (this time frame can be shorter if you believe you have subconsciously accepted your affirmation(s) and it has become "a part of you"). *Repetition of your affirmations is essential to your success.* Repeat your affirmations often, carry them with you, write them on a 3 x 5 card and post them on your mirror. Whatever works for you, DO IT!

5. Evoke as much emotion as possible when writing and verbalizing your affirmations. You must believe what you are affirming is possible.

6. Accentuate the positive in your affirmations. Never use negative words or phrases in your affirmations (such as I will not each chocolate cake anymore—this is counter productive and will not work).

7. Listen to spiritual, meditative or motivational music when writing and reciting your affirmations. Use the music that is right for you, but I highly recommend the largo sections from many of the Baroque composers from the 17th and 18th centuries (Vivaldi, Bach, Handel, Corelli, etc., or from a later period, Mozart). See *Affirmations Of Wealth – 101 Secrets Of Daily Success* for a full description of this method and specific musical selections.

In summary, affirmations, like prayer, must be part of our daily lives. In fact, our affirmations, and the time we spend declaring our worthiness through affirmations, is essential to our lives. These are by far the greatest methods to attune ourselves with God, stake our claim to our glory through Him and manifest the abundance that is ours by birthright.

Step 6: Trust in God.

This is easier said than done my friends. We are so full of human thoughts and emotions, and are so quick to trust in images and idols, that we have a tendency to put our faith in people first, principles second, and God last. We must certainly put our faith in people and principles, but we must reverse the order; faith in God first, principles second, then people. *In the most basic sense, we must surrender our will to God, refresh and regenerate our lives, and carve a new pathway to spiritual and financial freedom.*

How do we demonstrate our trust in God? We become fearless, remain faithful to the divine plan of our lives (although we may not see instant results), we accept the messages

God delivers to us and we put them into action. Trust is as much a function of action as it is a function of love. Are you willing to continue to do the right things to demonstrate patience when it is called for? Are you willing to be faithful to your calling, whatever that may be? Are you willing to give up loyalties to worn out conditions and worn out ideas? If you can answer "yes" to these questions you undoubtedly will demonstrate trust in God.

Step 7: Give gratitude continuously "now," before the manifestation of your dreams.

As you will see in the affirmations you are about to read, the two key words in this step are "gratitude" and "now." We must continually give gratitude now for the gifts we already have and for the one's we are about to receive. The manifestation process is not a bargaining process. It is a process of manifesting natural abundance in a divine way. We can't bargain with God or make promises we can't keep. There is no give and take with God. There is surrender, trust, humility, love, faith and gratitude. In order to manifest or have anything, we must demonstrate our belief that we shall have it and give thanks for it before the actual physical attainment of it.

In the truest sense, we do have everything now. We have the direction and love of God, the talents and gifts which are unique to us, the power and the right to stake our claim to our desires, and the physical or mental ability to carry them through until they manifest. This is what you must be grateful for, not the actual "things" you are about to receive, but the "gifts" you have already been given. Use your gifts. Mine your gold. Give thanks for all things now, and you shall have them.

Step 8: Use your intuition.

Our intuition is always right. This is a fairly easy conclusion to make since God is always right and always delivers us the perfect path for the manifestation of our desires, according to His plan. In one sense, intuition is a natural latent talent we each possess. Intuition can also be developed and fine tuned with experience and exercise. One of the most important intuition exercises is silence. Try this. Remain silent for 3 minutes. Find a quiet place, away from all distraction and noise. Close your eyes and remain silent. What do you hear? What words and images come to mind? What are your thoughts? At first, you may simply see and hear a jumbled mess. If you practice this exercise every day and expand the time you spend in silence by one minute each day (until you reach 30 or 60 minutes), your intuition will take over. You will clear the channel of worldly thoughts and make room for Godly thoughts.

Over time, you will begin to notice coincidences that correspond to your intuitive thoughts. You will see people who correspond with your thoughts who you haven't seen in months. People will begin delivering messages to you in their words and actions. Pay close attention. Sometimes these "bouts of awareness" you experience will not make sense in the immediate moment, but you will instinctively know, they contain a message for you. Try to write down your "hunches" and the directions of the small voice "in the back of your head." All of these messages are relevant to our lives, some how, some way. Use your awareness and bring these "coincidences" into your consciousness. They have been delivered to you for a reason. Your intuition can lead you in the right direction, help you make difficult decisions, keep you from harms way, help you form the right relationships, and keep you on the path to the manifestation of your dreams.

Step 9: Accept your directions and take action.

As a result of the first 8 steps of the manifestation process, you will see, hear and feel, intuitive or Godly messages. Don't judge these messages, trust them. Trust God and take action on them. If an action you take doesn't seem to serve any specific purpose, don't worry about it. You were meant to take that action to either learn a lesson, clear your channels, build your strength or to prepare you for the manifestation of your dreams. This is a very important step. *Don't pre-judge the method through whom, or the means by which, your dreams will manifest; take action.*

Step 10: Do all things with love. Be love in action.

Love what you do and do what you love. Dedicate yourself to the divine plan of your life and deliver love through your thoughts, your actions and your work. Become a servant in the truest sense of the word—a person who delivers love through humility for the furtherance of God's divine plan. *When you are love, deliver love, receive and accept love, you are prepared for the manifestation of your dreams.*

Step 11: Accept the manifestation of your dreams and goals.

This may sound like a silly step, but it is a step that many people cannot carry out. As you use this process, things will begin to manifest in your life; relationships, opportunities, material things, money. *When this happens you MUST accept them. If not, you will be denying God, denying God's love for you and you will diminish your self-worth. Accept everything that comes your way. These are divine manifesta-*

tions, they are signs of love and you deserve them. I cannot overemphasize this point: accept all the manifestations, gifts, love and money that gets delivered to you. These manifestations are the result of the true and honest use of your spiritual gold mind.

At first glance, the manifestation process may seem complicated. Read through the process again and you will see it is a natural process of love, awareness, faith and acceptance. It is actually fairly simple to understand and to use; *you can stop chasing after your dreams and goals and have them chase you!* Make this process, especially prayer, a stronghold of your every day life. Practice this process daily until it becomes a natural way of life for you, all the abundance and prosperity you have ever desired will be yours...if you accept it.

MONEY IS GOOD...
MONEY IS
GOD IN ACTION

*M*ONEY IS GOOD...
MONEY IS GOD IN ACTION*

The next several pages will be dedicated specifically to money. Even though you now understand the basic principles of manifesting wealth, you may still have a difficult time creating, accepting and proliferating money (keep in mind that money is different than wealth...money is cash and other forms of exchange). This is due to several reasons which I will explain as the *money laws. There are two types of money laws:* **laws of awareness and laws of application.** The money awareness laws are true and proven principles about money awareness and how this awareness, or lack thereof, plays an incredible role in the prosperity we attain in life. The money application laws are specific, tested and proven principles, that when adhered to, will lead to financial freedom. The money awareness laws and the money application laws are all grounded in spiritual principles. You have been using these laws for most of your life, they have affected your life for many years and will continue to do so for many more. Now however, with your new found awareness, the results you will manifest and see (as a result of the proper understanding and application of these laws), will be dramatically greater than any of the results you have created in your past.

*Eric Butterworth

The Money Awareness Laws

The money awareness laws are specific principles, spiritual in nature, which affect our consciousness and awareness of money, how we earn it, how we use it, what it represents to us, and how much we have of it. These concise laws will raise your consciousness about money to a much higher level. As a result, you will become aware of the money patterns in your life, why you have them, and if necessary, what you must do to change them. You will also notice a recommendation after each money law, which may be in the form of an exercise or illustration, to help you utilize each law and implement it in your life.

When reading the money awareness laws, you will have money memories and flashbacks, some of which may be very emotional. This is good, since bringing these memories into your consciousness will reveal the reasons why you may have had problems with money in the past. From here, with the use of the processes and exercises in this book, you can accept the past, remove any mental barriers you may have about money, and develop a new, healthier and prosperous money *gold mind.*

The Law Of Familiarity.

We tend to inherit the traits, tendencies, attitudes and beliefs of our parents about money. We each have a "money heritage," or genealogy, which can last for generations. We each also create the future money heritage of our families. We instill both our conscious and unconscious money beliefs in our children. Our children absorb our money "actions" as well. As a result of years of conditioning, our children tend to follow in our financial footsteps.

Recommendation:

Analyze your current savings, income and debt levels. Think back to when your parents were your age and try to recall (or ask them) what their savings, income and debt levels were. After adjusting for inflation, you may find your savings, income and debt levels, in terms of adjusted dollars, are within a few percentage points of your parents. Make up your mind today to establish the money heritage you want to pass on to your children, grandchildren and extended family. Then, do it.

The Law Of Consciousness.

The more awareness we have when saving, earning, investing or circulating money, the more we have of it. When we lose consciousness about money because of an addiction, the method we use to spend money, or indifference toward money, the less we have. I have already reviewed the affects of addictions on money depletion. But think about this for a moment: when we spend money with a credit (debt) card, over the telephone, while watching television, over the Internet or through some other type of electronic device, we do so "unconsciously." Because we are not physically handling cash, we tend to lose awareness of how much money we are spending and why we are spending it. This is a merchant's dream and your nightmare. Always stay conscious and aware of money in all forms. Money will tend to respond to your consciousness. If you have total awareness of your sources of income, money opportunities and the flow of money in your life, you generate and keep much more of it.

Recommendation:

When you spend or circulate money today, stop and look at the dollar (or whatever denomination) bills you are spending. Stop and think about why you are letting the money out of your life and ask yourself, "Is this a good investment?" Always stop and think before you spend. If you use a credit (debt) card or electronic commerce of any type, picture or visualize the cash leaving your hands as you charge the purchase. This will help you realize how much money you are actually spending.

The Law Of Responsibility.

Be responsible with your money. If you have thoughts such as, "well its only money," you are indicating a tendency to be irresponsible with it. Do the "little things" right with your money. If you are owed change from a purchase and it is "only a penny," don't walk away from it and leave it there. This is disrespectful. Deposit your money in the highest yielding accounts, even if the interest rate is only slightly higher. Call your credit (debt) card company and ask them to lower your interest rate. When you are responsible with (and to) your money, your money will respond accordingly.

Recommendation:

Take all of your "loose change" and deposit it into your investment or savings account. Start earning interest on it. This is just one way to train your subconscious mind to respect money and to train your money to respect you. Be creative. I am sure you can think of several more ways to accomplish this as well.

The Law Of Regeneration.

In order to generate more money, we need to regenerate ourselves. This is done through prayer, affirmation, visualization, love and gratitude. Refer back to the manifestation process for more insight on this. We must clear ourselves of past negative money experiences and fears in order to generate and keep money in our lives.

Recommendation:

Write down your most compelling money fear. Writing your fear(s) down on a piece of paper will help you "confront your fears." Then develop an affirmation, or use one of the *Affirmations For Spiritual And Financial Enrichment,* to help you overcome this fear.

The Law Of Simplicity.

The simpler we keep our lives, the simpler it is to attract money. Many of us tend to complicate our lives as some sort of "justification" mechanism. We tend to make things much more difficult than they need to be as some sort of test of our worthiness. Forget about this and simplify. If you use so much time and energy keeping your life complicated, you won't have the energy left to invest in making or attracting money, wealth, or love into your life. Keep things simple and you will have more money.

Recommendation:

Write down one way you can simplify your life today. Decide to "uncomplicate" your life by finding the simplest way to get things done.

The Law Of Attraction.

Money is attracted to people who have awareness of, respect for, and discipline when using money. We each can become "money magnets" by changing our awareness, our thoughts and attitudes, and by willingly accepting or assuming responsibility in our lives. Money tends to flow to people who have abundant and prosperous thoughts, who take prosperous actions, and who render service with or out of love. The "money chase" can be over for you if you change your attitude.

Recommendation:

You can begin attracting money into your life today. Visualize money (currency) flowing into your home, business and accounts. Give thanks to God for the good you have received. In a short period of time, if you use the other recommendations in this book, money will flow to you naturally.

The Law Of Acceptance.

In order to have more money, we must be willing to accept it. Many people get caught up in continually "denying" money. If someone offers you money, even if they are close friends or family members, graciously and gratefully accept it.

Recommendation:

Practice accepting and receiving gifts. Literally practice. Ask a friend to come to your house. Tell them about this book and that you are training your subconscious mind to be comfortable receiving money. Have them hand you money (cash) over and over. Keep taking the money and practice receiving it. This may seem silly, but this is a powerful way to build up your willingness to accept and attract money.

The Law Of Respect.

When we respect money, money respects us. The more respect we show to money, the more we have. Do you show spiritual, emotional and physical respect to your money? We must consciously respect money by doing the right thing, in the right way, at the right time, for the right reason with our money. We must be principle centered in our money thoughts and actions. When we do so, we get respect (money) in return.

Recommendation:

Make a list of the 3 previous choices you made about money. How did you earn, save, invest or spend it? Where these respectful and responsible choices? Do you do the right thing, at the right time, for the right reason with your money?

The Law Of Discipline.

Financial discipline is the surest path to financial freedom. Proper budgeting, investing and control of our money is one of the most liberating experiences in our spiritual and financial lives. When we are disciplined with anything, we eventually have more of it. Think about this for a moment. What do we have when we are more disciplined with our time? More time! What do we have when we are more disciplined with our eating and exercise habits? Longer, healthier, more abundant lives! The same principle holds true in every aspect of our lives. When we are disciplined with our money, the more we have.

Recommendation:

Make an honest evaluation of your income (after taxes) and spending levels. Reduce your spending to at least 10% below your income level (preferably 15%). Establish an investment account and invest the difference (if you have credit card debt, you would be better served using the additional money to pay off your credit cards rather than saving or investing). Don't even think that you can't do this because you can...it's a matter of setting priorities.

The Law Of Observation.

Always keep your money in sight. If you lose sight of your money, you will forget about it. *When we forget about money, it forgets about us and tends to take on a life of its own.* Those of you who have teenagers know what I mean. If you have a stock portfolio, check it every day. If you have account books, physically pick them up and look at them periodically. If you have cash in your home, keep it where you can physically see it or check on it regularly. Keep in mind, these are money "awareness" laws. In order to build financial wealth and the ability to attract money, we must train our subconscious to do so.

Recommendation:

If you have Internet access, build a stock portfolio and check it twice a day. You can do this with almost any "on-line" service. If you don't have Internet access, read the financial section of the newspaper today or subscribe to the Wall Street Journal. Make some "imaginary" stock picks and track them every day.

Take out your bank books or investment statements. Arrange them neatly, free from clutter and confusion. Each morning and evening, look at them.

The Law Of Maturity.

Spiritual maturity leads to financial and investment maturity. The more mature or "grown-up" we are, the more our money "grows." If we are immature in our thinking and our spiritual commitments, the less likely we are to gain financial independence.

Recommendation:

Write down one way you can "mature" spiritually. What commitment can you make to "grow up" spiritually? Make this commitment and watch your money grow.

The Law Of Indebtedness.

If we are spiritually, emotionally or physically indebted to anyone or any-thing, we tend to become financially indebted; our debt levels tend to be high or unmanageable. This happens, in many instances, due to a feeling of inadequacy, lack of self-worth (unworthiness) or guilt. I see this very often in family run businesses. If parents owned a business for many years and pass it on to their children, who don't really want to own or run this business, the children tend to have very high debt levels, spiritually, emotionally, physically and financially. Out of a sense of "loyalty" to their parents or family heritage, the children stay in the business only to develop low self-esteem, because they know, deep down inside, they would rather be doing something else. This is a cycle that continues to perpetuate feelings of guilt, and as a result, more debt.

Debts also tend to grow in our lives when we don't use cash. As simple as this seems, most people lose awareness of how much they are spending and continue to increase their debt as a result. Use cash as much as possible in your financial transactions.

Debts can also develop as a result of the "mental bank accounts" we keep.

We all tend to keep track, physically, of the "favors" we have done for people. We then "expect" them to do the same in return. If they don't, we get upset. Forget about keeping mental bank accounts, they are another form of debt accumulation. If you can't do this, start paying cash for "friendly" favors.

Recommendation:

Write down everything you "feel guilty about." List these items on a piece of paper. Then write next to each item, how this may have effected your financial life.

The Law Of Replenishment.

People who have a sense of giving, who continually give responsibly of their money to causes that are important to them, tend to attract more money into their lives. This is because man can be an outlet of both love and energy. *People who "give" with no expectation of anything in return, or "tithe" with the intention of replenishing the source of their money, make great investments of love.* We can each be great philanthropists in our way now matter how much money we give or tithe. Give and tithe money out of a sense of gratitude, love and glorification of God, not out of a sense of duty or obligation (this is just another form of psychic debt). When you give with gratitude and love, you open the channels for great abundance.

Recommendation:

Take the money out of your pockets right now. Take 10% of it and give it to a cause or charity that has a special meaning or sentiment for you. Even if this is only $1.00, give it with love. The love you will receive in return will be plentiful. Don't wait...do this now!

The Law Of Enthusiasm.

The word enthusiasm means "one with the energy of God," or "the God within." When we earn, invest and multiply our money with enthusiasm, we are doing so in a godlike manner. Genuine enthusiasm (not the phony stuff we see and hear so often), displays a genuine love for God, love for what we are doing, and love for other people. *When we are one with the energy of God, we are spiritually connected to everyone and everything. God is all encompassing, and you can be too. Be genuinely enthusiastic about the divine plan of your life and follow it faithfully. By so doing, you will automatically be filled with the energy of God, in all forms, including money.*

Recommendation:

Write down all the things that get you enthusiastic or the things for which you show great enthusiasm. Then ask yourself, "How can I convert my enthusiasm to profit?" Listen for the answer, then do it.

The Law Of Gratitude.

Of all the money awareness laws, I believe this is the most important. Developing and maintaining an attitude of gratitude about everything on our lives leads to the "flood gates opening." If you have a job you hate, remember you have this job as a result of your own choices. Give thanks that you have a job and a source of income. Continue to give gratitude and your attitude will change. Soon after, new opportunities will arise, new doors will open. Give thanks for those as well, then seize them and make them a real part of your life. Your gratitude for the good that you have will always lead to more good in the future.

Recommendation:

Verbally tell someone today you are grateful for their contribution to your life, then thank God as well. Make this a habit, then watch the flood gates open.

The Law Of Circulation.

Our money must always be in circulation or it becomes stale and loses its energy. When we circulate money, we circulate ourselves, our energy and our intentions. If we "hoard" money or treat it with disrespect, we block the flow of money circulating in our individual spiritual economies. Now this is not to say we shouldn't save or invest money. Keep in mind, when we are investing money, we are putting it to use. We are investing our energy, love and intentions in people and products that are, hopefully, doing the same thing (perpetuating this energy).

Keep circulating your money through responsible spending, loving charity, and spiritually mature investment decisions. Then your money will "pick up energy" and return to you multiplied.

Recommendation:

Write down the last time you experienced a "money blockage" and why you think you had this experience. Could you have avoided this through proper money circulation? How?

The Law Of Belief.

When our money travels, it takes with it our beliefs, attitudes and intentions. We literally "impress our mentality" onto our money and send our mentality to other people and places. This is a very important point. Always be aware of your attitude when releasing or circulating money. Your attitude, at the time you release (spend, give, invest) money, will have a dramatic effect on the results it will generate in the future. If you have thoughts of limitation at the time you release money, you will produce limitation in multiples for yourself and probably for other people. If you have thoughts of genuine enthusiasm, love, hope, charity and abundance when releasing money, you will produce the same in multiples as well. Remember, nature always compensates in multiples.

Recommendation:

Think about your day today. When you released money, what was your attitude? If your attitude was negative, change it now. "Re-send" thoughts of abundance and prosperity to the recipients of your money. If your thoughts while releasing money today were positive, congratulations. Nature will reward you.

The Law Of Love.

Bless your money, the Source of it, and the recipients of it, with love. Give with love, invest with love, circulate with love, and you will have love in great returns. You may not understand yet. I mean literally bless it. Make up a short blessing or prayer of love, prosperity and abundance. Send this spiritual message with your money, checks, etc., by reciting it when releasing money. *When we bless our money, we endow, consecrate or sanctify the receiver of it.*

I also recommend you keep your money (the cash, checks, etc., that you keep at home), in a blessed or sacred place. Where is the most spiritual place in your home? Prepare a place for your money there. *Keep aware, this is not to worship your money; idolatry can never be a part of your spiritual or financial life.* You want your money in a blessed or sacred place so it will carry blessings with it wherever it goes.

Recommendation:

Develop one way you can pass on your love with your money. Put this into action today.

By now, your awareness of money, and the various means of manifesting financial wealth, may be starting to shift. As you practice the money awareness laws, you will become one with the consciousness of God, in all aspects of your life, including your financial life. Your spiritual economy is beginning to take shape. You have all the tools necessary for financial freedom. Now let's go mine some gold!

The Money Application Laws

Now that you are "aware" of what money really is and how it acts and reacts in your life, you are ready to mine some gold. The money application laws are specific financial planning and manifestation principles that have been proven in the financial marketplace for years. In this section, you are going to learn how to apply these principles "in the real world" to garner specific financial gains.

The Earning Laws.

1. *Earn money honestly and with integrity.* If you earn money disingenuously, you will build up a devastating force of negative energy that will eventually ruin you spiritually and financially.

2. *Do what you love and love what you do.* If you love your profession, love

will spill over into every area of your life. Conversely, if you hate your job or profession, hate will spill over into every other area of your life. You must have the courage to live your dreams and live them now. Develop a responsible transition plan to follow your dreams, then they will eventually follow you.

3. *Money can and should "flow" to you from many different sources.* Income should "stream" to you as natural as a flowing river. There is a profession, career, investment(s) and/or opportunity's within your subconscious (gold) mind right now that will allow this to happen. Tap into your *gold mind* and put your ideas into action.

4. *Get in the habit of continuously receiving money whether you believe you "earned it" or not.* This money is flowing to you for a good reason.

5. *Always think and act like an entrepreneur.* Everyone is self-employed. Make yourself "invaluable" to your company and/or your clients and customers (and make no mistake about it, everyone is your customer). Go the extra mile in everything you do and do it with genuine enthusiasm. Every entrepreneur takes "ownership" in her company. You must do the same.

The Savings Laws.

1. *Money cannot save you, but you can save money.* Don't think of accumulating financial wealth as "savings." Think of it as an investment.

2. *Set aside the maximum allowable by law and invest it in your 401k, 403b or similar investment plan.* If you are self-employed, establish a profit sharing or simplified retirement (I abhor that word) plan and pay yourself first. Contribute to this plan every month. It doesn't matter at first what the amount is. Developing the habit of doing this is what counts.

3. *Save money regularly.* Aim for 10% of your after tax income or more (again, only if you have no credit card debt...if you have credit card debt, make it your top financial priority to pay that off first). If you don't think you have the money, cut your expenses. This is a matter of priority. What is more important, having

3 movie channels piped into your home for $30 a month or investing that money for your family?

4. *Have money direct deposited from your "paycheck" directly into an investment or savings account.* You won't miss what you don't see.

5. *Establish IRA accounts for your children immediately.* When your children begin to work, they can begin making the deposits. Teach your children the importance and discipline of saving and investing from the earliest age possible. The sooner you start, the easier this will be.

6. *Use time to your advantage.* Time has value and the time value of money is astounding. Stop wasting time and start investing both your time and money—now.

7. *Do not try to save money in your checking account.* Think about this logically for a moment. When money goes into your checking account, what is it actually doing? It is waiting to be spent! Deposit all your money into a savings or investment account. Only transfer money to your checking account when necessary to pay bills or large purchases when cash is not practical.

The Spending Laws.

1. *Use cash.* Cash is king in the financial world. This is the most "conscious" way to release money. Using cash keeps you aware of what you are actually spending.

2. *Spend 10% less than you currently do and invest the difference.* Don't tell me you can't do this. I know you can.

3. *Only use checks if you need a receipt or evidence of purchase.* Use checks to "pay bills" such as your mortgage, real estate taxes and regular household bills. For everything else, see #1 above. Using checks and credit (debt) cards are unconscious ways to release money. Whenever we release money unconsciously, we run the risk of accumulating debt beyond our immediate financial means. Checks should be used for business purposes or as a tracking mechanism.

Establish a "maximum" amount you can spend with a check without being accountable to someone else. If you need to write a check for more than that amount, stop and think first.

4. *Track every nickel you spend.* Every time you spend money, ask for a receipt or write down in a journal what you spent and why you spent it. ***This is probably the single most important thing I did to regain control of my financial life.*** For the past 3 and 1/2 years, I have tracked every nickel I have spent (on my computer). It takes me about 30 minutes a week to do this. It forced me to be extremely conscious of my spending habits and, as a result, I easily cut my spending by 15% while living a much wealthier lifestyle. Also, this method helps me budget and keeps great records in case of an audit (I was audited once and I won!). This may seem tedious but it really isn't. It actually becomes fun when you see how much of a profit or surplus you made each month.

5. *Credit (debt) cards should be used for identification purposes only.* If you use a credit card (notice I wrote card in the singular because you should not have more than one) to purchase an item, you must have a sufficient amount of cash available to "pay the bill" in full when you receive it.

6. *Do not purchase anything while watching television.* Almost everything you may buy while watching a shopping channel or an infomercial will be an "impulse" purchase. In other words, you will buy with emotion while your subconscious and conscious minds are under the control of someone else. If you see something you think is a "good deal," or an item you just "must buy," write down the telephone number of the company displayed on your television screen, but delay the call. Go to the local mall or discount store the next day and physically see and touch the item (or a similar one) you saw on television the day before. Investigate it closer and then make up your mind whether or not this is a good investment. Then make your best deal. Forget about those slick "buy lines" such as, "you must call now, there are only 5 left in stock." The next day you will see the same item on a different channel for the same or less money. Why are you watching so much television anyway?

7. ***Do not spend money over the telephone.*** See the explanation above. See, touch and feel things first, then buy them if they are a good investment or have sufficient entertainment value.

8. ***The Internet can be a fun place to shop, but I wouldn't want to live there.*** Electronic commerce is as much a form of entertainment as it is a source of products and services. Be careful here. You can view most products on the Internet. Deal with reputable companies or companies you have personal knowledge of. Always keep the awareness factor in mind. Are you making an impulse buy or a good investment with your purchase?

9. ***Always stop and think before you spend.*** Enough said. You get the point.

The Budgeting Laws.

1. ***You must have a budget.*** If you don't know how to make a budget, you can purchase (pay cash for it) any number of books on household or business budgeting. You can also purchase software programs that literally walk you through a few steps and create a budget for you. This should be done regardless of how much money you earn or spend.

2. ***Your budget should be done in monthly increments.*** Budget your income, expenses and savings, monthly. If you create a quarterly or yearly budget, it is too easy to let things slide and then try to make up for them later.

3. ***You must budget for savings (or debt reduction), investments and charitable donations.*** This is the surest way to insure you will save and invest a part of your income while still making the charitable contributions you want to make (remember again, paying off credit cards and personal loans should be your #1 priority before you begin saving or investing...make sure you budget for this). Make these items the first "expense" items in your budget. These are the type of expenses we like to have.

4. ***Build a "reserve" into your budget for emergencies.*** Some people may think this might just "invite" an emergency to happen. Wrong. When we budget

for emergencies we actually lessen the likelihood they will take place since we "already have them covered." Unfortunately, sometimes real life gets in the way.

5. *Be realistic when budgeting your income.* Many people tend to project more income then they are actually receiving. Be honest with yourself and your money will be honest with you.

6. *Budgeting helps establish the foundation for financial freedom.* Discipline is a habit which leads to freedom in all areas of our lives. Budgeting is simply one more freedom-manifesting habit.

The Gifting Laws.

1. *The tax advantages of gifting should be a secondary consideration.* Build charitable donations into your budget and pay them monthly. Do so because you truly want to help or give to someone or an organization in need.

2. *Make regular and consistent gifts.* Make charitable giving a habit and do it with gratitude.

3. *Investigate the charity fully before you give.* You have a responsibility to send your love and money to charitable organizations that are true in their intent of helping others or advancing a worthy cause, not advancing their own cause.

4. *If this is important to you, make sure your donation is tax deductible.* Many donations are not tax deductible. In my opinion, you should give anyway. This may be one of your greatest investments.

The Investing Laws.

1. *Make every investment similar to buying a new home.* When you buy a home, you usually look at many of them. Then you find the one that best fits your individual or family needs. After making the decision to buy, you hire professionals to inspect and investigate the property, physically and intellectually (title searches, etc.). You seek out the best financing rates and terms available

for you. Then you close the deal. You should use the same process when buying a stock, mutual funds, binds, insurance or any other type of investment.

2. *Invest in what you know.* When making financial investments, invest in products, investment vehicles or companies you are familiar with or have an interest in. For example, our twelve year old daughter Danielle loves to listen to music and watch movies. In her sample stock portfolio, after doing the proper homework, she recently invested in Sony. Her theory was, not only does Sony make and produce entertainment, they also produce the products, such as CD players and DVD's, that deliver the entertainment. She also determined that since it was near Christmas, sales would be strong this time of year, leading to more profits. I think this is a good long-term investment for her (as of the publication date of this book, Sony's stock value has increased 60%).

Our 15 year old son, Jarred, purchased Amazon.com. His rationale is that he likes the Internet and thinks it will be the primary electronic commerce vehicle of the future. Since Amazon.com is the world's largest online bookstore, it is natural to think they will expand into other services and products in the near future just like regular bookstores have (many have added software, audio's, music and other entertainment products). Jarred thinks Amazon.com might be both a place to shop and a source of entertainment in the future. Although the company is not profitable, the upside potential was worth the risk for him. Since he is 15 years old, he can afford to make higher risk investments (as of the publication date of this book, although it has been a volatile ride, Amazon's stock value has increased about 25%).

Our two other children, Jennifer and Erin, decided not to invest. *There is a very important lesson here. If you are not ready to do the homework necessary to invest, or to invest properly, don't do it.* They made a great investment decision by not investing at this time.

3. *Invest in principle centered companies or projects.* There are many companies who believe in and implement principle centered values in everything they do. You can tell this by the quality of their products, the quality of their people, and how they conduct their businesses. Ben & Jerry's would be a good example of

this. They include in their business plan financial provisions for community service, environmental enhancement, personal development for employees and their families, as well as a fair distribution of profits. In addition to all this, the ice cream is great! There are hundreds more companies that have the same principle centered leadership and goals. They maximize profits by adhering to principles not by conquering with a win-lose mentality.

4. ***Invest time.*** Invest time in your investments. Invest the necessary time, money and energy, researching, planning and analyzing your investments. Always do your homework.

5. ***Combine research with intuition for the best results.*** There are no idle hunches. If you have an instinctive or intuitive feeling about an investment, follow your intuition. Fully investigate the potential investment, then use common sense. If this investment makes good financial sense based on the facts, do it.

6. ***Invest time, energy and money in a proper estate plan, including life insurance and/or other types of necessary insurance.*** Since I practiced law for 13 years, this was an easy call to make. It is your responsibility to protect the future value of your estate and the emotional well being of your family. Don't leave them a mess to clean up if you pass on. Leave them a legacy of love, responsibility, and spiritual and financial freedom.

The Money Naming Laws

1. ***There are no "savings" accounts, only investment accounts.*** Your money is not there to "save" you. You don't "save" money as a method of saving your future or saving your soul. We invest money with the expectation of prosperous returns on our investments. Although I have periodically referred to "savings accounts" and "saving" money so far in this book, I have done so only because these are common terms most people understand. However, as you are beginning to understand, everything we do is an investment. If you view your accounts as "savings" accounts, you may create circumstances where you will "continually run to the bank" to be saved by your money. Take out your passbooks and

rename them to "investment" accounts, or something similar, that will exact a mental image of growth, prosperity and abundance.

2. *Retire rhymes with expire.* Rename your "retirement" accounts immediately. Choose a name which is fun and appropriate for you. You are not "saving for retirement," *you are investing for life.* Our subconscious, our *gold mind* within, knows the difference between retiring and living. Train your subconscious mind to deliver life to you, not retirement.

3. *Check means stop.* Rename your checking account to your "benefit account" or "flow account." The term "check" is a negative term. The core meaning of the word "checking" means to stop, arrest or barricade. You don't want to do this to your flow of spiritual or financial circulation. You are only going to use this account to pass on your blessings, in the form of paper money (checks), to other people or businesses.

4. *There are no credit cards.* Credit cards are simply a vehicle to accumulate debt. You may have noticed, everywhere in this book where I refer to credit cards, the word (debt) is always displayed as well. When you view your credit cards as debt cards, you will be less likely to use them.

5. *Rename your other accounts as needed.* If you have established specific accounts for specific purposes, be clever and creative in how and what you name this accounts. If you are setting aside money for your wedding, name this account, "The Love Account," or something similar. You get the point. Have fun naming your accounts. Your subconscious will have fun as well, and you will seek out and produce greater returns.

The Money Handling Laws

1. *Always circulate your money "the green side up."* Imprinted on the green side of US currency are the words, "In God We Trust." Pass on your "Trust in God" when you handle money. Always physically exchange money with these words facing up. You will be surprised who will get the message and what you will get in return.

2. *When you circulate money, pass on your blessings and wishes for prosperity to others.* Always bless the receiver of your money. When you do so, you establish the foundation of your personal blessings as well.

3. *Coins are money too.* Some people discard change (coins) like they are discarding junk. All money carries with it God's energy and your intended good fortune. If you don't want your coins, send them to me.

4. *Keep your money in a prosperous place.* Establish a place of prosperity for the money you keep in your home. This can magnetize your money to attract more money. Choose a bank or financial institution that has prosperous surroundings, prosperous minded employees, and an environment of wealth. If your bank or financial institution has "worn out" furniture and a "worn out" atmosphere, your money has "worn out" its stay there. Always do financial business in an atmosphere of prosperity. Prosperous conditions, coupled with a conscientious and skillful financial management team, is the atmosphere your money needs.

5. *Choose a financial advisor with a prosperous money heritage.* Ask the right questions of your financial advisor. Find out who they are, what their interests are, and what their financial background is. Get recommendations and clarify fee arrangements in advance. Be careful here. Remember that "like minds attract." If you have a history of being "reckless" with money, you may find a financial advisor who is reckless with money as well. Choose a financial advisor based on experience first, recommendations from existing clients second, their attitudes and beliefs third, the environment of their surroundings/office fourth, and fee structure last. A financial advisor who understands the prosperity principles will always ask you about:

    a) Your short term and long term financial and personal goals.

    b) Your past money experiences and your money heritage.

    c) The legacy you want to create for yourself and your family.

    d) Your personal, family and professional interests.

    e) Your money patterns (attitudes and beliefs).

If a financial advisor spends most of the appointment talking about his or her company; selling you on the merits of his/her company's products and what they can do for you, find someone else, you are in the wrong place.

The Tax Laws

A study of the actual tax laws is well beyond the scope of this book. I am not a tax expert or CPA. There are a few basic rules you should follow however. For everything else relating to taxes, hire an expert.

1. *Always pay your taxes and pay them on time.* Hire a professional to prepare your taxes, file them on time, and pay your estimated taxes regularly. Delaying payment of taxes is just another subtle way to burden yourself with both financial and emotional debt.

2. *Never cheat on your taxes, you are only cheating yourself.* If you cheat on your taxes, you probably will cheat on other things as well. Sooner or later we all learn, we never actually cheat anyone else out of anything; we only cheat ourselves of self-respect, dignity and integrity.

3. *If you need help with your taxes, get it....but remember, you get what you pay for.* If you do hire a professional tax expert, invest a few dollars more if necessary and hire an expert who knows what they are doing.

The money application laws are slight-edge techniques that can and will dramatically enhance your financial performance and the manifestation of your financial dreams. But the money laws will only work for you if you put them to use. Schedule and plan time to prepare a comprehensive financial strategy for yourself and your family. The framework has already been established for you... you are now "well aware" of the power of these financial laws and strategies. The only person that can prevent your financial independence at this point is you. For your sake, for your family's sake, and for God's sake, put these laws into action now.

Money And Couples

The bond between husband and wife is a bond created by God's love and their love for each other. Love is at the center of both spiritual fulfillment and financial freedom. It is with love that all couples, whether husband and wife or loving partners, should establish the foundation of financial success and freedom. When money becomes a problem in a relationship, it is never "the money" that causes the problem. The opposite also holds true; when there is great love and happiness in a relationship, it is not because of money. In order for a couple to be financially rich, they must be rich in all areas of their joint lives. There must be a commonality of spirit, a physical bond and love, coupled with mutual financial goals, dreams and desires. If money is the driving force in any relationship, instead of God and love, financial freedom can never be attained. God and love must always be the Source of all abundance. Here are some suggestions for couples who want to manifest their financial dreams and goals.

1. *You must work together for the love of God.* Your relationship is a confirmation of God's love. Pass this love on jointly to other people.

2. *Pray together.* Pray together, and as a family. Your collective love and gratitude can do wonders for you spiritually and financially.

3. *You must support each other's goals and uplift each other continually.* There have been more people "broken" as a result of the indifference of their spouse or partner, than by any corporate raider or business competitor. Work together, not against each other.

4. *You must develop a collective consciousness about money.* Just as we must "move into consciousness" with God to attain spiritual fulfillment, every couple must move into a collective financial consciousness to attain financial freedom. If one person (or both) remains loyal to an addiction, a worn out paradigm, or cannot clear the channels of financial manifestation and prosperity by releasing the past (through forgiveness), a cloud of spiritual and financial uncertainty will always veil their partner.

5. *Make a financial commitment born out of love for God, love for each other, and love for your family.* Have the courage to let go of worn out conditions and worn out things. Do an honest self-evaluation and admit your shortcomings to your partner. Then dedicate love and patience to each other, and work together to manifest your dreams and a family heritage of wealth for future generations.

6. *Respect each other's individuality, but never become an individual.* When one partner in any relationship decides to be an individual rather than enrich their individuality through the strength of a relationship with God and their partner, a collective consciousness cannot be established or maintained, spiritually or financially. Be individually strong but collectively stronger.

$\mathscr{S}$PIRITUAL & FINANCIAL
SELF-DISCOVERY
CHECKLIST

✑PIRITUAL & FINANCIAL SELF-DISCOVERY CHECKLIST

Answer these questions honestly and truthfully prior to reading the *Affirmations for Spiritual and Financial Enrichment.* After completing this checklist, you will have established the foundation necessary for developing your goals and affirmations. The truths revealed to you while completing this checklist may also help you gain some insight for the journalizing portion of the affirmations in the "Thoughts," and "Actions," sections. For many of you, completing this checklist will be a very emotional exercise, but keep in mind, this is an essential step in manifesting your financial freedom.

1. What is your greatest spiritual strength? _____

_____

_____

_____

2. What is your greatest spiritual weakness? _____

_____

_____

_____

3. If you only had one year to live, what spiritual commitment would you make?

_____

_____

Why? _____

_____

_____

_____

Why aren't you doing this now? _____

_____

_____

Should you be doing this now? _____

_____

4. Do you believe in God or A Higher Power? _____

_____

If your answer is yes, how do you practice your faith, religion, spirituality and beliefs regularly?

_____

_____

5. Do you pray or meditate regularly? _____

_____

Why or why not? _____

_____

_____

If your answer is yes, how do you pray or meditate? _____

_____

_____

Why? _____

_____

_____

Does this feel natural to you? _____

_____

Why or why not? _____

_____

Could you improve this? _____

How? _____

_____

_____

6. Do you carry on a continual conversation with God? _____

Why or why not? _____

_____

If not, how could you do this? _____

_____

7. Do you feel worthy of God's love? _____

Why or why not? _____

_____

_____

If not, what does your intuition tell you is the reason for this feeling of unworthiness?

_____

_____

_____

What does your intuition tell you about how to overcome this feeling of unworthiness?

_____

_____

_____

8. Do you fear God? _____

Why or why not? _____

_____

_____

If you fear God, does this enhance or diminish your life? _____

Why? _____

_____

_____

How? _____

_____

_____

How will you improve this? _____

_____

_____

9. What is your image of God? _____

_____

How did you form this image or belief? _____

_____

Does this image of God enhance or diminish your life? _____

Why? _____

_____

_____

How? _____

_____

How will you improve this? _____

_____

_____

10. Have you ever felt you were in the palm of God's hands? _____

When did this happen? _____

_____

Where were you? _____

_____

Why did this happen? _____

_____

_____

Can you relive these moments? _____

How? _____

_____

_____

11. Describe the most extraordinary spiritual experience you have ever had.

_____

_____

_____

Why was this so extraordinary? _____

_____

_____

_____

_____

12. How do you channel God's love to others? _____

_____

List all the ways you can channel God's love to others in each role of your life (spouse, parent, child, sibling, friend, business person, employee, employer, etc.)

_____

_____

_____

_____

_____

13. If you are a Christian,* how do you follow Christ* (how are you Christ*-like)?

_____

_____

*Muslim - Mohammed - Mohammed-like? _____

_____

_____

*Buddhist - Buddha - Buddha-like? _____

_____

_____

Please complete the appropriate references for your faith or way of life.

How has this enriched your life spiritually? _____

_____

How can you improve upon this? _____

_____

_____

14. What is the source of your greatest spiritual strength?_____

_____

Why? _____

_____

_____

15. What does wealth mean to you? _____

_____

_____

16. Who has influenced you the most regarding your beliefs about...

Your faith and spiritual life? _____

_____

Money? _____

_____

17. Has this influence been positive or negative?_____

Why? _____

_____

_____

Do you need to change this? _____

_____

Why and how?_____

_____

_____

_____

_____

18. Do you love God?_____

Why or why not?_____

_____

_____

19. Who do your trust more, God or yourself?_____

Why?_____

_____

_____

20. Do you believe God has a divine plan for your life?_____

Why or why not?_____

_____

_____

If not, what do you believe? _____

_____

_____

Why?_____

_____

_____

21. Do you consider yourself to be an ethical person? Explain your response...

_____

_____

_____

_____

_____

22. What is the greatest spiritual investment you have ever made?

_____

Why?_____

_____

_____

What was the return (or the expected return) on your investment? _____

_____

23. Are you happy with the quality of your life?_____

If so, why? _____

_____

_____

If not, why not?_____

_____

_____

How will you improve upon this? _____

_____

_____

24. What is your greatest financial strength?_____

Why is this your greatest financial strength? _____

_____

_____

How can you improve upon this? _____

_____

_____

25. What is your most limiting financial weakness? _____

_____

Why is this your most limiting financial weakness? _____

_____

_____

How can you improve upon this? _____

_____

_____

26. What are the sources of your income right now? _____

_____

Why are these the sources? _____

_____

If you could change these sources, would you? _____

Why and how? _____

_____

_____

What attitudes or beliefs created these as the sources of your income? _____

_____

Do you need to change your attitudes and beliefs about yourself (or something else) and/or make a new spiritual or financial commitment to improve upon this?

_____

If so, what must you do? _____

_____

_____

When and how are you going to do this? _____

_____

_____

27. How much is your income right now? _____

List each source of your income and the specific amount. _____

_____

_____

Why is your income at this level? _____

_____

What attitudes or beliefs led you to create this as your income right now?

_____

_____

Do you need to change your attitudes and beliefs about yourself (or something else) or make a new spiritual or financial commitment to improve upon this?

_____

If so, what must you do? _____

_____

_____

When and how are you going to do this? _____

_____

_____

28. What do you want your annual income to be? _____

Why? _____

_____

If this is so important to you, why isn't your income at this level now?

_____

_____

What spiritual and financial commitments do you have to make to raise your income to this level?

_____

_____

How and when are you going to do this? _____

_____

_____

29. Has your income grown over the past 3 years?_____

Why or why not?_____

_____

_____

If not, is there a spiritual or financial commitment you could have made that would have allowed your income to increase? _____

If so, why didn't you do this?_____

_____

What can you do to improve this? _____

_____

_____

30. What is the balance(s) in your checkbook(s) right now? _____

Why is it at this level? _____

_____

_____

Should your balance(s) be different? _____

What attitudes or beliefs helped you create this as your checkbook balance at this time?

_____

_____

Do you need to change your attitudes or beliefs about yourself (or something else) and/or make a new spiritual or financial commitment to improve upon this?

_____

If so, what must you do? _____

_____

_____

When and how are you going to do it? _____

_____

_____

31. What is the balance in your savings account(s) right now? _____

Why is it at this level? _____

_____

Should your balance(s) be different? _____

What attitudes and beliefs helped you create this as your savings account balance(s) at this time?

_____

_____

Do you need to change your attitudes and beliefs about yourself (or something else) and/or make a new spiritual or financial commitment to improve upon this?

_____

_____

If so, what must you do? _____

_____

_____

When and how are you going to do this? _____

_____

_____

32. How much cash do you have in your possession and/or in your home right now?

_____

Should you have more or less cash? _____

What attitudes or beliefs helped you to create this as your cash on hand at this time?

_____

_____

Do you need to change your attitudes or beliefs about yourself (or something else) and/or make a new spiritual or financial commitment to improve upon this?

_____

If so, what must you do? _____

_____

_____

When and how are you going to do this? _____

_____

_____

33. What financial investments do you have right now?

List each investment and the dollar value of each?

_____

_____

_____

Why do you have these particular investments? _____

_____

What attitudes or beliefs helped you to create these as your investments at this time?

_____

Should your investments be different? _____

Why? _____

_____

_____

Do you need to change your attitudes or beliefs about yourself (or something else) and/or make a new spiritual or financial commitment to improve upon this?

_____

If so, what must you do? _____

_____

_____

When and how are you going to do this? _____

_____

_____

34. What are your credit (debt) card balances right now? _____

List each credit card and the existing balance. _____

_____

_____

_____

Why are your credit (debt) card balances at this level? _____

_____

_____

What attitudes or beliefs helped you to create these as your credit (debt) card balances at this time?

_____

_____

Do you need to change your attitudes or beliefs about yourself (or something else) and/or make a new spiritual or financial commitment to improve upon this?

_____

If so, what must you do? _____

_____

_____

When and how are you going to do this? _____

_____

35. What are your other financial debts or obligations (personal loans, taxes, credit purchases, etc.) right now?

List each additional financial debt or obligation.

_____

_____

_____

Why are your financial debts and obligations at this level?_____

_____

What attitudes or beliefs helped you create these as your financial debts and obligations at this time?

_____

_____

Do you need to change your attitudes or beliefs about yourself (or something else) and/or make a new spiritual or financial commitment to improve upon this?

_____

If so, what must you do? _____

_____

_____

When and how are you going to do this? _____

_____

_____

36. Do you love your career(s) or profession(s)? _____

If so, why? _____

_____

If not, why not? _____

_____

What attitudes or beliefs helped you to create this as your career or profession at this time?

_____

_____

Why did you choose this as your career or profession? _____

_____

_____

If you "had it all to do over again" what would you have chosen as your career or profession?

_____

Why? _____

_____

_____

37. If money was not an issue in your life, what career or profession would you choose or create?

_____

Why? _____

_____

_____

Can you create this career or profession now (even if it is only to a limited degree)?

_____

How can you do this? _____

_____

_____

What spiritual or financial commitment must you make to help you create this career or profession?

_____

_____

When are you going to do this? _____

_____

_____

38. Do you have a financial advisor right now? _____

If so, why? _____

_____

If not, why not? _____

_____

Should you have a financial advisor? _____

Does your financial advisor have a prosperous mentality? _____

Why or why not? _____

_____

List the prosperous traits of your financial advisor. _____

_____

_____

List the prosperous and spiritual traits you would like your financial advisor to have.

_____

_____

Does your financial advisor know and understand your
spiritual, financial and family goals? _____

Why or why not? _____

_____

_____

Does your financial advisor know your money heritage? _____

Why or why not? _____

_____

_____

Should you reveal your money heritage to your financial advisor? _____

Why or why not?_____

_____

Should you change financial advisors? _____

Why or why not? _____

_____

If so, to whom and why?_____

_____

39. Do you own life, disability, health, long term care or other types of insurance?

_____

List each of your policies and why you own each one. _____

_____

_____

Are you "over insured" or "under insured?" _____

When was the last time you had your policies reviewed?_____

Are they sufficient to meet your current spiritual, family and financial goals? _____

Do you have an estate plan (will, living trust, etc.)? _____

If so, what does your estate plan consist of?_____

_____

_____

When was the last time you had your estate plan reviewed? _____

Is it sufficient to meet your current spiritual, family and financial goals? _____

If not, should you have an estate plan?_____

Who should you contact about this? _____

_____

Have you been "delaying" doing this? _____

Why? _____

_____

How and by when are you going to do this? _____

_____

_____

40. Do you use a bank or other financial institution right now? _____

Which bank(s) or financial institution(s) are they? _____

_____

How much money do you have on deposit with each institution? _____

Why? _____

_____

Does the physical appearance of the bank(s) or financial
institution(s) you use display a prosperous mentality? _____

Why or why not? _____

_____

Do the employees and/or the management of the bank(s) or financial
institution(s) you use display prosperous mentalities? _____

Why or why not? _____

_____

Should you be using another bank or financial institution (or should
you consolidate your accounts into one bank or financial institution)? _____

Why or why not? _____

_____

_____

If so, what actions are you going to take and when? _____

_____

_____

41. Do you own stock in a particular company or companies? _____

List each company, how many shares you own and why you own them.

_____

_____

What values do the management, employees and directors of this company deliver to the spiritual economy?

_____

Are these values congruent with both your spiritual and financial beliefs? _____

If so, how? _____

_____

_____

If not, why not? _____

_____

_____

Should you continue to "own stock" in these companies? _____

Why or why not? _____

_____

_____

42. Do you own any mutual funds or other equity-type investments? _____

List each fund/investment, its current dollar value, and why you own each one.

_____

_____

What values do the management, employees and directors of these companies/ investments deliver to the spiritual economy?

_____

Are these values congruent with both your spiritual and financial beliefs? _____

If so, how? _____

_____

_____

If not, why not? _____

_____

_____

Should you continue to "own" these funds / investments? _____

Why or why not? _____

_____

_____

43. Are you paid current on your federal, state and local taxes (personal and, if applicable, business taxes)?

_____

If you are "delinquent" on your taxes, list each tax owed, the amount and to which governing authority they are owed.

_____

_____

What attitudes or beliefs helped you create this as your current tax situation?

_____

_____

_____

Do you need to change your attitudes or beliefs about yourself (or something else) and/or make a new spiritual or financial commitment to improve upon this?

_____

If so, what must you improve upon? _____

_____

_____

When and how are you going to do this? _____

_____

_____

44. What "emotional debts" do you have right now (do you feel like you "owe" things to other people)?

_____

_____

What do you think you owe to other people and to whom do you think you owe it? List each person or entity you think you owe something to and what you believe you owe them.

_____

_____

_____

What attitudes or beliefs helped you create these "thoughts of indebtedness?"

_____

_____

Do you need to change your attitudes or beliefs about yourself (or something else) and/or make a new spiritual or financial commitment to improve upon this?

_____

_____

If so, what must you improve upon? _____

_____

_____

When and how are you going to do this? _____

_____

_____

45. If someone tries to give you money, how do you respond? _____

_____

Is your instinct to accept money or deny it? _____

Why is this your instinct?_____

_____

What attitudes or beliefs helped you to create your instincts or acceptance or denial of money?

_____

_____

Do you need to change you attitudes or beliefs about yourself (or something else) and/or make a new spiritual or financial commitment to improve upon this?

_____

If so, what must you improve upon?

_____

_____

When and how are you going to do this?

_____

_____

_____

List the specific actions and the date by which you will take them.

_____

_____

46. If someone tries to give you a gift, how do you respond? _____

_____

Is your instinct to accept or deny gifts? _____

Why is this your instinct? _____

_____

What attitudes or beliefs helped you to create your instincts about the acceptance or denial of gifts?

_____

Do you need to change your attitudes or beliefs about yourself (or something else) and or make a new spiritual or financial commitment to improve upon this?

_____

If so, what must you improve upon? _____

_____

_____

When and how are you going to do this? _____

_____

_____

List the specific actions and the date by which you will take them.

_____

_____

_____

_____

47. How do you "feel" when you "spend" money? _____

_____

List all the emotions and thoughts you experience when "spending" money.

_____

_____

Why do you feel this way? _____

_____

_____

What attitudes or beliefs helped you to create these "feelings" about "spending" money?

_____

Do you need to change your attitudes or beliefs about yourself (or something else) and/or make a new spiritual or financial commitment to improve upon this?

_____

If so, what must you improve upon? _____

_____

_____

When and how are you going to do this? _____

_____

_____

List the specific actions and dates by which you will take them.

_____

_____

_____

_____

48. After reading the following truth, would your
answer to question number 47 change? _____

When I am spending money I am investing in the spiritual economy. _____

_____

When I lovingly, consciously and wisely circulate money, I am passing on God's
flow of goodness to many other people.

_____

How would your answers change, and why? _____

_____

_____

49. What is your first money memory and how has it impacted your life (what is
the first thing you remember about money and why do you remember this)?

_____

_____

Is this a positive or negative memory? _____

Why? _____

_____

_____

50. What is your money heritage (what financial traits or characteristics have you
inherited from your parents, particularly about money)?

_____

_____

In what ways have these characteristics either enhanced or limited your financial
situation?

_____

_____

Does your money heritage continue to enhance or limit
your financial life and wealth? _____

Why and how? _____

_____

_____

Do you need to change your attitudes or beliefs about yourself (or something else)
and/or make a new spiritual or financial commitment to improve upon this?

_____

If so, what must you do? _____

_____

_____

When and how will you do this? _____

_____

_____

List the specific actions and dates by which you will take them.

_____

_____

_____

51. Do you experience "money blockages" (times when
money just won't flow to you)? _____

Why does this happen? _____

Can you become more aware of these things while they are happening? _____

How can you do this? _____

_____

_____

52. Do you invest your time wisely? _____

If your answer is yes, how do you invest it wisely? _____

_____

If your answer is no, why don't you invest it wisely? _____

_____

How can you improve upon this and by when will you do it? _____

_____

_____

Do you see time as an expendable resource or as a finite asset that has a growing value?

_____

Why? _____

_____

Do you understand the time value of money
(the effect time has on the growth of money)? _____

How much is your time worth on an hourly basis? _____

How did you determine your answer? _____

_____

Why did you determine it this way? _____

_____

How much is your "free" time worth? _____

How did you determine your answer? _____

_____

Why did you determine it this way? _____

_____

53. Do you have any addictions* that prevent you from reaching your true financial potential? _____

What is your addiction(s)? _____

How does your addiction interfere or hinder your financial success and/or the financial situation of your family and business (employment)?

_____

_____

How much money do you spend or lose to your addiction on a weekly basis? _____

What spiritual, financial, emotional, physical or family commitment must you make to overcome this addiction?

_____

_____

What specific actions are you going to take and by when are you going to take them?

_____

_____

What professional help will you seek or employ to overcome your addiction?

_____

By when and how are you going to do this? _____

_____

_____

*Be aware that addictions can be very subtle. Caffeine, nicotine, watching too much television and overeating can be as devastating as alcohol, gambling, sex or drug addictions. Be honest with yourself.

54. List all the creative ideas you have about making money?

_____

_____

_____

How long have you had these ideas? _____

Have you acted on these ideas? _____

If so, how and why? _____

_____

If not, why not? _____

_____

Can you put these ideas into action soon? _____

How are you going to put them into action. _____

_____

_____

Do you need to change your attitudes or beliefs about yourself (or something else) and/or make a new spiritual or financial commitment to put these ideas into action?

_____

List the specific actions and date by which you will take them.

_____

_____

55. Describe, in detail, the life you would lead if you had all the money you ever desired.

_____

_____

_____

_____

_____

_____

_____

In detail, map out your typical wealthy day.

What would you do? _____

_____

_____

Where would you go? _____

_____

_____

With whom would you do these things? _____

_____

Why? _____

_____

_____

What would you buy? _____

_____

_____

Why would you buy these things? _____

_____

_____

What else would you do with your money? _____

_____

_____

How and why? _____

_____

_____

56. If you had $1,000,000 more than you currently have right now, what specifically would you do with it?

In detail, list exactly what you would do with it, when you would do it, how you would do it, and why?

How would this enhance your life, the lives of other people, and glorify God at the same time? Be specific.

_____

_____

_____

_____

_____

_____

_____

_____

_____

_____

_____

_____

_____

_____

_____

_____

_____

_____

AFFIRMATIONS FOR SPIRITUAL & FINANCIAL ENRICHMENT

*A*FFIRMATION:

My happiness is God's affair, therefore I Am released from the tyranny of fear.

*N*ARRATION:

Much can be said in a few words. There are several lessons in this affirmation. Let's first start with the word's "My happiness." In order to develop a prosperous mentality and to receive all the goodness that is intended for us, we must first believe we have the right to be happy. So many people feel guilty about being happy or, simply don't believe they deserve to be happy, that they shut out abundance, prosperity, God and many wonderful relationships (as a result of their "undeserving," or "lack" attitudes). ***God didn't create us to be poor in spirit. He created us to be rich in spirit.*** Your happiness is God's affair and it is your affair as well. You deserve to be happy and you are obligated to be so. You cannot do God's work carrying guilt, sadness, lack or limitation.

As you read in my book, *Affirmations of Wealth – 101 Secrets of Daily Success,* the only thing that ever prevents us from manifesting our dreams and fulfilling our individual destinies in life is fear. Releasing ourselves from the grip of fear is a fundamental step in the manifestation or accomplishment of any goal or dream. What are fears anyway? They are only *thoughts!* Change your thoughts and you will change your life forever. Repeat often, "I Am released from the tyranny of fear," or, ***"I Am fearless,"*** and surely your fears about all things will begin to fade away.

WISDOM FOR TODAY:

Date_____

Today I will face my fears. I know my happiness is God's affair and I deserve to be happy. When I face my fears and allow them to fade away, I clear the channel for my intended good fortune.

SCRIPTURE REFERENCE:

"The Lord is my helper, and I will not fear what man shall do unto me."
Hebrews 13:6.

THOUGHTS: _____

_____

_____

_____

_____

_____

_____

ACTIONS: _____

_____

_____

_____

I am fearless™

AFFIRMATION:

*Money is Good...Money is God in Action!**

NARRATION:

I can hear some of your thoughts now. How dare he equate money with God. There is a very important lesson in this affirmation; **God's flow of energy is in everything!** We are an expression or extension of God. So are the trees, your home and the car your drive. Money is an ever present reality in life. You can make it a natural part of your life, a natural extension of who you are, or you can deny it and suffer from the lack of it.

So many of us have been taught for so long that "money is the root of all evil," or people with money are, "greedy" or "bad," that we have lost the truth about money. Money is neither good or bad. Your thoughts and actions about money are either abundant or negative. If you think and act negatively about money, you will repel money from your life. If you think abundantly about money and what it can do for you and others, it will naturally flow into your life.

Forget about the excuse that, "money isn't everything." I have heard that excuse a thousand times. This is just one more way to avoid the responsibility of creating abundance in your life. If money isn't important, why do you have any? You could live without it. You could live in the park and walk everywhere you go. You could get free clothing at a shelter and free food. You don't really need money do you? ***Money is God in action.*** Most people who do not have money either have a fear of money and the happiness it can bring into their lives, have a hidden envy or jealousy of people who have money, or have an irresponsible attitude toward what money can help them create in life (or how money can help them carry out God's divine plan). The fact is money isn't everything, but ***your thoughts and attitudes about money are.*** Forget about the excuses and change your thoughts about money. When you appreciate money, you appreciate God. When you accept money, you accept God. When you freely spend and give money, you pass on God's abundance. When you do good with money, you do good for God.

*Eric Butterworth

*W*ISDOM FOR TODAY:

Date_____

Today I view money as a natural part of my life. I appreciate what money can do for me and what I can do with money. I erase the old tapes that play negative thoughts about money and I affirm the goodness of money.

*S*CRIPTURE REFERENCE:

"And God blessed them, and God said unto them, 'Be fruitful, and multiply, and replenish the earth'..." *Genesis 1:28*

*T*HOUGHTS: _____

_____

_____

_____

_____

_____

_____

_____

*A*CTIONS: _____

_____

I am fearless™

*A*FFIRMATION:

Prosperity and Abundance are mine now and forever...each day I wake up to new wealth.

*N*ARRATION:

The most important word in this affirmation is **NOW**. Prosperity, abundance and money are not things that you have to chase after. They are already here for you to accept. Look all around you and what do you see? Natural expressions of God's abundance is everywhere. You see a beautiful reflection of God in nature. You see people going about their daily lives. You see business people and businesses creating wealth. The prosperity and abundance is already there for you, but *you have to accept it as a natural part of your life now.*

In its truest sense, prosperity, abundance, living an abundant life and accepting the material manifestations of abundance (money, homes, etc...) are choices. Can you accept the prosperity that is intended for all of us and can you accept it as part of your life now? If you can at least begin to believe that you deserve these things, you will begin to accept and receive them *now.*

Each day, accept the wealth that is intended for you that day. If the wealth comes in the form of an extra hour to take a walk, accept it. If it comes in the form of a smile from your neighbor, accept it. If it comes in the form of money, accept it. When you deny wealth, you deny God's flow of abundance. When you accept wealth, you accept God's flow of abundance. Accept it *now.*

*W*ISDOM FOR TODAY:

Date_____

I clearly see God's abundance in all things. I see that they are here now. Today, I stop chasing and start accepting the wealth that is here for me.

*S*CRIPTURE REFERENCE:

"Let us go up at once and possess it; for we are well able to overcome it."
Numbers 13:30.

*T*HOUGHTS: _____

_____

_____

_____

_____

_____

_____

_____

*A*CTIONS: _____

_____

_____

I am fearless™

*A*FFIRMATION:

I Am always in the Harvest Ground.

*N*ARRATION:

There is a fundamental law of nature, a spiritual law that simply states; *we reap what we sow.* The most important thing any of us can sow are our thoughts. Our thoughts and attitudes are everything. The relationships we have in our life are a result of our thoughts. The amount of money we have in our bank accounts are a true reflection of our thoughts. *Our external world is an astonishingly accurate reflection of our inner world* (our thoughts, beliefs and attitudes). If we have confusion, doubt and lack in our outer world it is because we have confusion, doubt and lack in our minds, and most likely in our relationship with God. The external world always reflects and reacts to our inner world. If you have peace, clarity and abundance in your inner world, your outer world reflects the same.

Wouldn't it be wonderful to live in the Harvest Ground all the time? What images appear in your mind when you think of the harvest? Harvest fairs, a sense of accomplishment, a sense of completeness, the material things you can purchase with the money from the harvest? You already are in the Harvest Ground. You already reap what you sow. In order to harvest abundance, you must sow abundance. In order to reap material things, you must sow material things. You must plant them in your mind, protect and nurture those thoughts. You must water them and weed them. Then, you will harvest all good things.

Change what you plant and you will change what you harvest. Plant abundance, prosperity, God's goodness, and all the desires you have in the fertile soil of your mind. This is the beginning of the harvest that will surely enrich your life.

WISDOM FOR TODAY:

Date_____

Today I plant and sow only thoughts of abundance, prosperity and wealth. I protect and nurture these thoughts from the storms of negativity that may appear from time to time. As I think, I Am. I think abundance, I Am abundance.

SCRIPTURE REFERENCE:

"Be not deceived; God is not mocked: for whatsoever a man soweth, that shall he also reap." *Galatians 6:7.*

THOUGHTS: _____

_____

_____

_____

_____

_____

_____

_____

ACTIONS: _____

_____

I am fearless™

AFFIRMATION:

I Am full of perfect ideas which bring perfect results.

NARRATION:

Our ideas, attitudes and beliefs are our greatest assets. The amazing thing most people don't realize is that we are all full of perfect ideas. It is your job to let them out and put them to use to manifest your destiny. Napoleon Hill once stated, **"There has been more gold mined from the minds of men then in all the gold mines in the world."** Mr. Hill is exactly right. Every thought you think has a seed of opportunity in it. This is one of God's greatest gifts to mankind...our ability to think, our ability to choose, and our ability to take action on our choices.

Your mind is abound with perfect ideas. Ideas on how to improve something or create something. Ideas on how to better your life or the life of someone else. Ideas on how to glorify God. Ideas on how to make money. Your intuition is always right. Trust your intuition. When you trust your intuition, you are trusting God. Trust is always reflected in actions. If you truly trust God and have faith, you will act on the ideas that have been delivered to you. If you only put faith in how other people will perceive your actions, you do not trust in God. It is your obligation to succeed regardless of what other people say, think or do. Your results, no matter what they may seem to you or others, are always perfect results, when you act as an expression of God's will.

God is love and God is perfection. You are an expression of God. Deliver God's absoluteness through your actions and you truly are perfect.

*W*ISDOM FOR TODAY:

Date_____

I Am a perfect expression of God today and I demonstrate my faith through my actions. With God, all results are perfect—no matter how I perceive them.

*S*CRIPTURE REFERENCE:

"Choose you this day whom ye will serve." *Joshua 24:15.*

*T*HOUGHTS: _____

_____

_____

_____

_____

_____

_____

_____

*A*CTIONS: _____

_____

_____

I am fearless™

*A*FFIRMATION:

I Am a player in the great game of life. I Am always in the game.

*N*ARRATION:

What a precious gift we have been given. We can through prayer, visualization, affirmation and subconscious direction, create whatever we want to be, do or have in life. Then we can consciously choose to have it. Life doesn't get much better than that! But in order to manifest these things in life, we must be in the game. We can't be sitting on the sidelines, watching life go by as we watch television. Come on. Don't you get it yet? ***Every day is a new opportunity to create good, to have fun, to work for the glorification of God, to learn new things and to live a life of fulfillment.*** Those among us who do not have this attitude must ask ourselves, "why not?" The answer to this simple question will reveal the path to your freedom, spiritually, physically, emotionally and financially.

What is holding you back from prosperity, abundance, wealth and the manifestation of your dreams? It may simply be, you are not in the game. How do you get into the great game of life? You trust in God. You take control of your own mind. You become a doer instead of a watcher. You accept wealth as a natural part of life and you accept the truth that you deserve to have it now.

Forget about surviving and start living. Thoughts about surviving lead to actions of surviving. Thoughts about living lead to actions of prosperity.

WISDOM FOR TODAY:

Date_____

Today I get in the game and I begin to live. If I get knocked down, I get back up and I live some more.

SCRIPTURE REFERENCE:

"Don't be fools; be wise: make the most of every opportunity you have for doing good." *Ephesians 5:16.*

THOUGHTS: _____

_____

_____

_____

_____

_____

_____

ACTIONS: _____

_____

_____

I am fearless™

AFFIRMATION:

I Am blessed with Divine enthusiasm; I follow the perfect plan of my life.

NARRATION:

Divine enthusiasm is a metaphor for "God in action." In order for any of us to have divine enthusiasm, we must be following God's intent and purpose for us. It is no wonder so many people are not happy. I recently read a statistic in the Wall Street Journal; between 50% and 80% of the workforce in the U.S. is unsatisfied with their jobs and wish they could be doing something else. WOW! What a statement about lack of faith. I am always amazed when I read that 90% of the population believes in God yet only 20% act like they believe in God. If you act with divine enthusiasm you will discover the perfect plan of your life. It might not be the exact plan you perceived it was going to be, but it is a perfect plan nonetheless.

God is pointing the way all the time. But you must be willing to follow God's divine plan for your life. The people in our country who are fabulously wealthy, are the people who have developed a passion for the direction and natural gifts God has given them. What is the perfect plan for you? Ask God. You will get an answer. You may not like the answer, but you will get one. If you want to be wealthy, follow the plan.

When you are following the perfect plan of your life, you are an open channel for the natural abundance intended for you. Abundance will flow naturally and honestly to you in all forms and manifestations. I can hear some of you now. There are thoughts going through some of your minds such as, " My perfect plan is to be a teacher (or something else) but I can't make any money at it." Forget about that scarcity mentality. There are many teachers who are financially independent (but their money comes from a different source). Here is the "secret." *Money comes as a result of who you are, how truthfully you are following your plan and what you do with your opportunities.* Money does not necessarily come as a result of your chosen profession.

Decide today to follow the divine plan of your life and your riches will surely come.

WISDOM FOR TODAY:

Date_____

I have the courage to follow the divine plan of my life. I forget about scarcity and begin to act prosperously, knowing that my plan is a perfect expression of God's love for me.

SCRIPTURE REFERENCE:

"For I know the plans I have for you, " declares the Lord, "plans to prosper you...to give you hope and a future." *Jeremiah 29:11.*

THOUGHTS: _____

_____

_____

_____

_____

_____

_____

_____

ACTIONS: _____

_____

_____

I am fearless™

AFFIRMATION:

God is my Supply...I DESERVE TO BE wealthy.

NARRATION:

The affirmative belief, I DESERVE TO BE, is the essence of wealth, abundance and prosperity. Think carefully for a moment. Look at the word DESERVE. Look up this word and its origin in the dictionary. The word DESERVE means **to be of service.** So when you affirm the words I DESERVE TO BE you are expressing your acceptance to serve God and to serve other people. Let's look at these affirmations for a moment.

I DESERVE TO BE wealthy. This affirmation confirms you are wealthy as a result of the service you render to other people.

I DESERVE TO BE happy. This affirmation describes your happiness as a result of the accomplishment and fulfillment you feel as a result of serving other people.

I DESERVE TO BE healthy. This affirmation describes your physical and mental health as a result of the service you give. When you render service with a true purpose of serving God, as you are serving others, you are always healthy.

The most prominent obstacle to most people's financial wealth, happiness and healthy lives are their beliefs that they don't deserve to have these things. Now that you know the true meaning of the word DESERVE, it is easy to see that we all deserve to be wealthy in every aspect of our lives. Use this affirmation often. **When you believe you deserve to be, do and have all things, you will be, do and have all things.**

WISDOM FOR TODAY:

Date_____

I Am entitled to and worthy of all good things. I render service for God and for others. I receive marvelous returns.

SCRIPTURE REFERENCE:

"To be the greatest, be a servant." *Matthew 23:11.*

THOUGHTS: _____

_____

_____

_____

_____

_____

_____

_____

ACTIONS: _____

_____

_____

I am fearless™

$\mathcal{A}$FFIRMATION:

Money flows easily to me for the good of all concerned.

$\mathcal{N}$ARRATION:

One limiting mindset many people have is that there is a limited amount of prosperity or money to go around. Many people think, "If I have more money, someone else will suffer." This is either an old nonsensical thought that has been littering your subconscious for many years, or it is an excuse not to accept the responsibility that comes with having more money. Either way, these thoughts are fundamentally incorrect.

There is more prosperity, abundance and financial wealth in our world than any of us could ever conceive. The amount of loose change that falls out of people's pockets every day is enough to make you a multi-millionaire. Take the natural wonders of the world for example. They never get depleted. Niagara Falls has millions of gallons of water flowing over it every few seconds, but it never goes dry. Money can flow as easily and abundantly to you, just as naturally as the water flows over Niagara Falls. One fundamental belief you must accept and hold is *when wealth and money flows to you, it is for the good of everyone.* You have rendered a valuable service, or given a valuable idea, or performed valuable labor for it, and now it belongs to you.

Forget about the old limiting idea that you must "work hard" for your money. What a bunch of hooey. What you must do to have any amount of money you want is to believe you deserve it, that it is a natural expression of God's love for you, and that you have rendered a valuable service, thought or idea for it. When you are willing to accept this truth you will be able to accept, manage and proliferate your wealth. If you think you must "work hard for the money," forget about it. Start working hard for God with your abundant thoughts, your abundant ideas and your abundant service.

WISDOM FOR TODAY:

Date_____

Today, I accept the good that comes my way. When money flows to me it is a natural result of my goodness.

SCRIPTURE REFERENCE:

"My God will supply every need of yours according to his riches."
Phillipians 4:19.

THOUGHTS: _____

_____

_____

_____

_____

_____

_____

ACTIONS: _____

_____

_____

I am fearless™

ᴀFFIRMATION:

There is power in simplicity. I always find the simplest and most divine way to get things done.

ᴀRRATION:

Why do we try to make things more complicated than they really are? It seems many of us feel we need to justify our existence by busily filling our time with wasteful and useless thoughts and actions. When you think about most things in life, they really are simple. Start thinking of your time and what you do with it, as well as your actions and what you do with them, as divine time and divine actions. *If God were looking over your shoulder and giving you regular progress reports, wouldn't you be more productive and less wasteful with your time, money and energy?* God is looking over your shoulder, you just can't see Him (unless you are really looking, of course).

Here is what all things are made of:

Love   Energy   Time

Use all of these assets wisely and simply. Do all things with love. Invest and reserve your energy divinely (with an intended good purpose). Value your time as much as you value God, love, and all other good things you respect and admire. Schedule your time effectively, use it efficiently, and give it deservedly. *Simplify all that you do. Find the easiest and most effective way to get things done, and low and behold, you will get things done.*

*W*ISDOM FOR TODAY:

Date_____

Today, I simplify my life by applying my love, energy and time wisely.
When I simplify my life, I create more room for prosperity.

*S*CRIPTURE REFERENCE:

"Do what is right in the sight of the Lord, so that it may go well with you..."
Deuteronomy 6:18.

*T*HOUGHTS: _____

_____

_____

_____

_____

_____

_____

_____

*A*CTIONS: _____

_____

_____

I am fearless™

AFFIRMATION:

A share of all I earn is mine to keep.

NARRATION:

I have seen this affirmation also expressed as, "A part of all I earn is mine to keep." But, since the word *share* is a financial term, and is also a term that can mean service, I decided to use *share* instead of "part." If the affirmation, "A part of all I earn is mine to keep," feels better to you, then by all means, use that affirmation.

I often am asked to help people who make a lot of money but never seem to be able to keep any of it. There are many people who are great at earning or manifesting money, but for some reason, never seem to have any. As a matter of fact many of these people make a substantial amount of money, but their debt level rises faster than their income. Why does this happen? Again, we go back to the fundamental beliefs we have about ourselves first, then to the beliefs we have about money.

If we believe we are deserving, we keep our money and save, spend, gift and invest it wisely. If we feel undeserving, guilty, envious or limited in our lives, we do whatever we can to "get rid" of money. When we spend more money than we make or accumulate debt to support our spending habits, we are reflecting our inner feelings of guilt, unworthiness or fear. Silly thoughts like, "What are people going to think if I have more money," and "This money is going to change me," begin to creep into our minds.

Keeping a share of all that you earn is a necessary and crucial step in developing financial wealth. Keeping a share of all that you earn builds self-respect, builds confidence, and establishes a subconscious pattern of saving. No matter what your income level is, save a share of it. This will lay the foundation for your financial freedom.

WISDOM FOR TODAY:

Date_____

Today, I think before I spend. I consciously keep or save a share of all that I earn. This is one of the first steps to my financial freedom.

SCRIPTURE REFERENCE:

"...every man should eat and drink, and enjoy the good of all his labor, it is the gift of God." *Ecclesiastes 3:13.*

THOUGHTS: _____

_____

_____

_____

_____

_____

_____

_____

ACTIONS: _____

_____

_____

I am fearless™

AFFIRMATION:

I Am prepared for the manifestation of my financial success.

NARRATION:

Florence Scovel Shinn described this concept succinctly and powerfully in her book, *The Game Of Life And How To Play It.* In life, we have many unanswered prayers. Many people think this is true because they aren't asking correctly, God sees them as undeserving, or they are not persistent enough in their prayer. All of these are "religious" fallacies that stagger our faith. *The truth is we don't typically get what we pray for, we get what we prepare for.* Now don't get me wrong. I am a big believer in the power of prayer. Prayer is one of the focal points of my life. Prayer helps us find inner peace, it gets us in touch with God, it lets our intentions be known to God and through God, and prayer reveals the answers to our appeals. Prayer also helps us to develop an attitude of gratitude which is necessary for the manifestation of our desires.

But receiving the answers to our prayers is wrought with emptiness unless we are prepared to harvest the results through our actions. Dorothea Brande, in her great work, *Wake Up And Live,* described prayer as thought coupled with action. She revealed the secret to the manifestation of our dreams through prayer in the metaphor, "When you pray, move your feet." In other words, *you must physically and mentally prepare* for the manifestation of your dreams through prayer.

In order to be, do and have all things, you must be prepared for them, you must accept the responsibility that comes with them, and you must be willing to carry them out. If you pray but are not prepared for the manifestation of your prayers, dreams and goals, they surely will not manifest. Prepare for financial freedom, prepare for success, prepare to accept God's greatness in all its forms, and then you shall have them.

WISDOM FOR TODAY:

Date_____

Today I will follow my prayers with actions. I will demonstrate my willingness to accept wealth by preparing for it.

SCRIPTURE REFERENCE:

"And five of them were wise, and five of them were foolish. They that were foolish took their lamps, and took no oil with them." *Matthew 25:2,3.*

THOUGHTS: _____

_____

_____

_____

_____

_____

_____

_____

ACTIONS: _____

_____

_____

I am fearless™

*A*FFIRMATION:

Everything I do is profitable.

*N*ARRATION:

In its truest sense, the word profitable means, "to advance", "to gain" or "fruitful" (to multiply). Here come the questions. I can hear them. "What do you mean everything I do is profitable? The last time I invested in the stock market, I lost money." Now stop and think for a moment. You may have temporarily lost some money, but what did you gain?

There is certainly something to learn from everything we do. Continually ask yourself the question, "What did I gain from this transaction (relationship, experience, challenge, etc.)?" Then take the profit from your experiences and make them fruitful.

"Well," you say, " it can't be that easy. I have to beat myself up first, then do a complete analysis of the entire world economy, then I have to blame someone or something else for my loss." Listen closely, there is no loss and there is no one else to blame. No amount of analysis will resolve a past decision. Ask yourself, "What did I learn from this experience?" Everything you do and think is profitable some how, some way. Did you gain experience? Did you advance beyond a prior way of thinking? Then you profited.

In the financial sense, the word profit means you made money. And, if you put the recommendations in this book to use, you will make money. *Keep in mind however, making money is a result of our belief systems, our attitudes and our choices.* If you believe you deserve financial gain, you have the proper attitude about financial gain and you make choices consistent with those beliefs, then everything you do will be profitable.

*W*ISDOM FOR TODAY:

Date_____

I realize the return on all my investments of time, money and energy are a reflection of my own choices. If I don't like the results I am getting, I must change my attitudes, beliefs and choices.

*S*CRIPTURE REFERENCE:

"The Eternal God is thy refuge, and underneath are the everlasting arms."
Deuteronomy 33:27.

*T*HOUGHTS: _____

_____

_____

_____

_____

_____

_____

*A*CTIONS: _____

_____

_____

I am fearless™

*A*FFIRMATION:

My income continually increases whether I Am at work, at sleep or at play.

*N*ARRATION:

You have made it to the Promised Land. Can you believe it? You are making money 24 hours a day, 7 days a week, 365 days a year! The fact is, this is a way of life for all people who have a prosperity consciousness. How can this be true? How can I make money if I am not working? Well, let's examine this thought for a moment. If you have a savings account or any other type of deposit account that pays interest, regardless of how low the interest rate is, you are making money 24 hours a day—you are continuously making money.

If you are continuously making money on your savings account, why can't you do this in other ways as well? The answer is you can. Think about this for a moment. You are reading this book. It doesn't matter where you are or when you are reading it. At the moment you purchased the book, you created income for the publisher, the distributor, the printer, the graphic artist, and the people who supply the materials such as the inks and the paper. You created income for the shipping company who shipped it to the local bookstore. You earned a profit for the bookstore owner and the employees of the store. You created income for the author and for the author's assistants such as the editor and bookkeeper. You created a revenue stream that paid taxes for the benefit of many people and you enhanced an economy from which hundreds of people benefited, including yourself, because you bought the book. Now, at the time you bought the book, with the exception of the bookstore employee(s), none of these people were physically "working."

Yet all these people profited.

You can profit 24 hours a day as well. In many respects, you are right now. Seek new ways and new opportunities to generate income for you, your family, and for the benefit of others. When you do, you spur a spiritual economy into action—God's love, divine plan and goodness are put into action for the benefit of many people.

*W*ISDOM FOR TODAY:

Date_____

I Am making money all the time. The amounts of money I make are a reflection of my own attitudes. I now know abundance and prosperity are part of the spiritual economy. God cannot fail, so I cannot fail.

*S*CRIPTURE REFERENCE:

"Now glory be to God who by his might power at work within us is able to do far more than we would ever dare ask or even dream of." *Ephesians 3:20.*

*T*HOUGHTS: _____

_____

_____

_____

_____

_____

_____

_____

_____

*A*CTIONS: _____

_____

_____

I am fearless™

Affirmation:

Success is the natural way. I Am successful.

Narration:

Here is where I differ from many of the "metaphysicians." Many people will tell you there is no success, there is only a state of being. Can you understand that? I can't understand it. I know, based on my previous experiences, how I feel when I accomplish certain things. I know what it feels like to experience success and to experience failure. It is never my goal to disassociate myself from these feelings. It is my goal to feel and "be" successful.

I also know from scripture, from experience, and from looking at nature, that success is a natural process. Abundance is a natural process. Prosperity is a natural process. If a farmer plants one grain of wheat, what does he get in return?... Hundreds of grains of wheat. If a teacher plants an idea, what does she get in return?... Hundreds of ideas and thoughts. *Nature always compensates in multiples and so does God.* If we think negatively, our negative thoughts produce multiple negative results. *If we think positively, we produce multiple positive results.*

The same process holds true with money. If we attract money to ourselves in a negative or wrong manner (or we don't feel good about the way we earned it), that money, and the thoughts that attracted it, will produce negative results, maybe forever. If we attract money spiritually, positively, and with positive thoughts and actions, our money will produce positive results forever.

*W*ISDOM FOR TODAY:

Date_____

I Am successful today because I think and act positively. I know these positive thoughts and actions will multiply and create a natural flow of success in my life and in the lives of other people.

*S*CRIPTURE REFERENCE:

" For as man thinketh in his heart, so is he..." *Proverbs 23:7.*

*T*HOUGHTS: _____

_____

_____

_____

_____

_____

_____

_____

*A*CTIONS: _____

_____

_____

I am fearless™

AFFIRMATION:

I always have a prosperous mind...I always have extra money.

NARRATION:

"It doesn't seem like I always have extra money." Was that your first response when you read this affirmation? If so, let's dig a little deeper here. As I heard Frederic Lehrman state on his tape series, *Prosperity Consciousness,* "If you have any money with you at all, you have extra money." Keep in mind there is a difference between money and obligations. Our subconscious mind knows the difference but sometimes our conscious mind forgets this. Money is cash in any form: dollar bills, coins, gold and silver. Our obligations are pieces of paper which remind us of our choices.

For example, on your desk or counter at home, you may have some notices reminding you to pay for the cable television bill or your phone bill. You will pay these bills, probably with pieces of paper as well (checks). Money is something completely different. Money is the physical manifestation of cash and other tangible things that we can use. It is our intent, with this affirmation, to help you create more money in the tangible form.

The balances in your bank accounts and investments are a representation of the amount of money you have earned and saved, not necessarily the amount of paper you have received. When thinking about money, think in terms of cash and tangible items. Remember, we get what we prepare for and what we focus on. If you focus on money, in terms of cash and other tangible items, that is what you will get. We can convert the cash later into investments, homes, cars and the like, but for now, focus on money and how to attract it to you.

The goal is to have a healthy balance of money expressed in tangible terms such as cash, as well as money in the abstract such as investments, checks, certificates of deposits, etc. Don't "forget" about money and the importance of having a healthy amount of money/cash in the tangible form. Having money/cash helps keep you free from some forms of debt such as checks to cover, credit cards and promissory notes.

*W*ISDOM FOR TODAY:

Date_____

Money is a natural part of my life. I keep tangible forms of money with me at all times. I don't rely on debt, I make choices with cash.

*S*CRIPTURE REFERENCE:

"If thou return to the Almighty, thou shalt be built up, thou shalt put away iniquity far from thy tabernacles. Then shalt thou lay up gold as dust, the gold of Ophir as the stones of the brooks. Yea the Almighty shall be thy defense and thou shalt have plenty of silver." *Job 22: 23-25.*

*T*HOUGHTS: _____

_____

_____

_____

_____

_____

_____

_____

*A*CTIONS: _____

_____

I am fearless™

AFFIRMATION:

I have no debt...there is no debt in divine mind.

NARRATION:

This is an extraordinarily powerful affirmation. When using this affirmation, you must be prepared for the results. When you start to clear your mind of debt (the residue of past choices) and move into divine mind (a world of perfect abundance), many things will begin changing in your life. Unfortunately, many of us resist change. We feel we are losing our identity or we fear change itself. Quite honestly, many of us need to lose our financial identity.

This affirmation clears the channel for tremendous abundance. When we release debt, we release old patterns of negativity and guilt about money. When we release debt, we release a part of the past. When we release debt, we let go of many emotions and choices. *But releasing tangible debt (bills, credit cards, etc.) and psychic debt (indebtedness to family tradition or the ideals of others) is a necessity to gain prosperity.*

Even though we all say we want to be debt free, the numbers on our credit card statements don't reflect this. Nor do our increased bills and obligations, both real and psychic. Amazing things will happen when you use this affirmation. Here are some real examples. When I started to use this affirmation, I had substantial credit card debt which was costing me financially and emotionally. Several months later, it was paid off. Within a few weeks of using this affirmation, I received notice of a parking ticket that I was issued two years previously. I do not remember getting this ticket, but I was at the location described in the notice on the date the ticket was issued. You see, I desired to be debt free and the debts I needed to release were brought into my conscious world, *as well as the means to release these debts* (I now had the mental and tangible means to pay off these debts).

Have faith when using this affirmation. You will manifest the subconscious debts that are lingering in your mind, but you will also manifest the means to release those debts. Surely the answers and the means to release your debts will come.

WISDOM FOR TODAY:

Date_____

Debt is a worn out condition in my mind. I no longer need debt for any reason. All is square.

SCRIPTURE REFERENCE:

"...let us throw off everything that hinders...let us run with perseverance the race marked out for us." *Hebrews 12:1.*

THOUGHTS: _____

_____

_____

_____

_____

_____

_____

_____

ACTIONS: _____

_____

_____

I am fearless™

AFFIRMATION:

Every dollar I release returns to me multiplied.

NARRATION:

We pass on our energy in many different forms. One way is through our thoughts, another way is through our actions. When we pass on money, we are also passing on our energy. When we gift, spend or invest money, our mindset is extremely important. We actually can and do "impress" our mentality onto the money, checks, credit cards, debit cards, e-commerce transfers and any other means of releasing money. This is an extremely important point.

Our mentality travels with our money and our money travels with our mentality. When we release money with a scarcity mentality (our thoughts are negative and focused on limitation or the reasons why we shouldn't be spending the money), we create more scarcity for ourselves and for others. When we release money with a prosperous mentality (we joyfully are spending the money with a good intent and we are focused on the abundance the money will produce), we create prosperity for ourselves and others. The same law holds true for giving or tithing. I have seen many people give or tithe money with an expectation of something in return or for personal gain or recognition. When this is done you have wasted your money and you have passed on negative energy to the organization or person you "donated" to. If your donations are nothing more than tax deductions, keep your negative energy to yourself, don't curse the organization with your scarcity.

Remember that our thoughts are eternal; they continue to produce results forever unless we consciously shut them off. So "impress" your money and other forms of exchange with blessings of abundance and abundant thoughts. Every time I release money or pay a vendor, I silently affirm, "Go forth and multiply...create abundance for many."

Pass on your good wishes for divine abundance to all. Do this with truth and a sincere wish for prosperity for all people who come in contact with your energy. When you are sincere in heart and mind when releasing money, it will come back to you in plenitude.

*W*ISDOM FOR TODAY:

Date_____

Today I Am conscious of my thoughts when releasing money (or other forms of exchange). I pass on my blessings and wishes for abundance when I release money (or other forms of exchange) and I receive a multitude of abundance in return.

*S*CRIPTURE REFERENCE:

"Every day I will bless you." *Psalm 145:2.*

*T*HOUGHTS: _____

_____

_____

_____

_____

_____

_____

_____

*A*CTIONS: _____

_____

I am fearless™

*A*FFIRMATION:

God is prosperous so I Am prosperous.

*N*ARRATION:

God is the omnipotent energy of spiritual fulfillment and total abundance. If you are experiencing lack or limitation in your life, it isn't God punishing you or testing you; your station in life is a result of your personal choices. God doesn't create negative circumstances to test you. We attract them to ourselves through fear, self-doubt, envy and jealousy. When these thoughts are "cast off" and we release ourselves from these useless emotions, we begin to live a life of prosperity.

Stop and think about this for a moment. *The universe is constantly expanding. Nature is constantly renewing itself and growing. There is evidence everywhere that we live in an abundant universe—it's all around us. God is abundance. God is prosperity.* The only way we can prevent prosperity and abundance from our lives is if we either consciously or subconsciously deny it.

God doesn't hold envy in His heart. God has no fears or self-doubts. God has no jealousy. Therefore, neither should we. We are an expression of God and His goodness. Only man, through negative thoughts and actions, can deny abundance and prosperity.

Eliminate your lack thoughts and focus on God and His ever present love and abundance. Remember, you get what you focus on and what you prepare for. Focus on God and prepare for prosperity and your life will change forever.

WISDOM FOR TODAY:

Date_____

Today I Am aware of the total abundance in me and around me. I see God in all that I do and all that I see. God is unlimited and so Am I.

SCRIPTURE REFERENCE:

"But seek ye first the kingdom of God, and his righteousness; and all these things shall be added unto you." *Matthew 6:33.*

THOUGHTS: _____

_____

_____

_____

_____

_____

_____

_____

_____

ACTIONS: _____

_____

_____

I am fearless™

AFFIRMATION:

I continually attract what I want from life and I let the rest go.

NARRATION:

Prosperity, abundance, money, material things, our purpose in life, do not come as a result of us "chasing after them." All the things we want to do, be and have come to us when we stake our claim to them and then exercise our faith to allow them to manifest.

We are like magnets. We each have these incredible abilities to attract to ourselves what we want from life, but most of us never use this power.

Life will give you exactly what you demand or claim. You have exactly what you have right now, and you are what you are, because you have declared it (or, believe it or not, we have allowed someone else to declare it for us). Every day we each are declaring our scarcity or abundance, lack or joy, emptiness or love. We declare these things in our thoughts (affirmations and statements of belief) and in our actions or lack thereof.

Make an inventory of the things you must let go: your thoughts, your old beliefs, your feelings of guilt about past thoughts or actions, material things that are now useless or worn out. Get rid of them. *When you release your past burdens you renew yourself, just as nature does. You clear the channel for acceptance and attraction.* You now may stake your claim to the abundance which is yours by birthright. You now can focus on the present and use your creativity and energy to manifest all of your desires.

WISDOM FOR TODAY:

Date_____

I let go of worn out ideas and worn out beliefs. I Am a magnet for abundance, joy and happiness.

SCRIPTURE REFERENCE:

"Be renewed in the spirit of your minds, and put on the new nature."
Ephesians 4:23,24.

THOUGHTS: _____

_____

_____

_____

_____

_____

_____

_____

ACTIONS: _____

_____

_____

I am fearless™

AFFIRMATION:

I see every possibility and act on every opportunity.

NARRATION:

Our minds have more power than all the computers in the world. We can create a vision of what we want our lives to be and we can manifest it, almost immediately, if we really believe it is possible. ***Our intuition and our ability to visualize are powerful tools in attracting abundance and in maintaining our faith.***

If you are having some difficulties in determining your path in life, there is a simple solution. Go to a quiet place where you can be free from all distractions. Close your eyes and count backwards from twelve to one (you may want to have soft music playing in the background. See my book, *Affirmations of Wealth – 101 Secrets of Daily Success*, for a more in-depth explanation of this method). Picture these numbers before you as you count backwards. After you get to the number one, ask God for the solutions or answers to that which you are seeking. After a few days of practice, you will be amazed at what appears. Visions and thoughts will come very clearly to you.

Here is the major point: ***you must accept God's direction and act upon it.*** There will be names, places, pictures and hunches that you will receive. Don't ignore these. The answer to your prayers "is not out there." The answers to your prayers are inside of you. When you receive your answers, don't judge them. Who are you to second guess God? Keep holding these pictures and thoughts in your mind. These pictures and thoughts are your vision of the "unseen" that you need to keep your faith. Act, act, act on the messages and the opportunities you have been given, and trues riches will be yours.

𝒲ISDOM FOR TODAY:

Date_____

I see clearly and act with faith. All my answers are within me.
I Am free from judgment and full of understanding.

𝒮CRIPTURE REFERENCE:

"Your ears shall hear a word behind you, saying, 'This is the way, walk in it'..."
Isaiah 30:21.

𝒯HOUGHTS: _____

_____

_____

_____

_____

_____

_____

_____

𝒜CTIONS: _____

_____

_____

_____

I am fearless™

𝒜FFIRMATION:

I Am what I affirm.

𝒩ARRATION:

The words **"I Am"** are divine. When you declare your **I Am - ness,** you are declaring your sacredness. God is the almighty. God revealed Himself to Moses as the **"I Am."** We all need to express ourselves as the **I Am,** as well. *When we declare a thing in the I Am sense, we are declaring our unlimited strength, our all-powerful selves, our faith and our belief in the Almighty.* That is why the words I Am are so important in affirming our beliefs.

Look at the following affirmations and then reflect how you feel after reading them. Express your feelings in writing in this book or in a journal. Your divine self and your oneness with God are always declared with the words, **I Am.**

I Am fearless.

I Am a person of value under God.

I Am a contribution.

I Am a divine expression of God's love.

I Am abundance.

I Am worthy of all good things.

$\mathcal{W}$ISDOM FOR TODAY:

Date_____

Today I reflect on the abundance and joy that is within me. **I Am** *fully aware of my oneness with God and I affirm my divine self.*

$\mathcal{S}$CRIPTURE REFERENCE:

"Evening and morning and at noon will I pray, and cry aloud, and He shall hear my voice." *Psalm 55:17.*

$\mathcal{T}$HOUGHTS: _____

_____

_____

_____

_____

_____

_____

_____

$\mathcal{A}$CTIONS: _____

_____

_____

_____

I am fearless™

𝒜FFIRMATION:

I Am in the flow...I work with life, not against it.

𝒩ARRATION:

So many of us work against the natural order of life it is no wonder we have so much illness and deprivation in the world. Can you imagine being "in the flow" or "in the zone" all of the time? Can you think of the times you were completely happy in your life and everything was going your way? This can and should be the natural way in life.

For some reason when things begin to flow smoothly and we are experiencing abundance, prosperity and material gain, many of us "shut it off" and go back to the old mentality.

In order to develop riches in our lives, including money, we need to be in the flow. If we are constantly battling against nature, we are going to lose. *It is natural to be happy, healthy and rich.* We are working against the flow in life when we experience sadness, illness and lack. When we are poor of mind, we are poor of heart as well. Don't let the "nay-sayers" convince you otherwise.

There is no room in the divine mind, nor is there room in the spiritual economy, for doubt, fear, lack thoughts or perceived limitations. There is only room for abundance, fearlessness, fulfillment, joy, love, gratitude and divine presence. Focus on these things and on getting in the natural flow of life. Use your intuition to guide you. Engage in a continuous conversation with God. Ask God for the guidance to keep you moving with the flow. When you begin to struggle in life, stop and ask yourself, "Why is this happening now?" Then simply listen for the answer, and if you must, change course and get back in tune with God.

*W*ISDOM FOR TODAY:

Date_____

I do not have to struggle today spiritually, physically, emotionally or financially. I find the most natural path and I follow the divine plan.

*S*CRIPTURE REFERENCE:

"But the fruit of the Spirit is love, joy, peace, patience, gentleness, goodness, faith, meekness, temperance: against such there is no law." *Galatians 5:22,23.*

*T*HOUGHTS: _____

_____

_____

_____

_____

_____

_____

_____

*A*CTIONS: _____

_____

_____

_____

I am fearless™

*A*FFIRMATION:

I Am always in the Promised Land.

*N*ARRATION:

It never ceases to amaze me when I hear comments like, "I know if I sacrifice now, God will reward me by delivering me to the Promised Land." Sacrifice what? *Here is one of the major keys to financial freedom; you are already in the Promised Land. There already is abundance, peace, prosperity, love, happiness, joy, wealth and serenity around you, and more importantly, in you.*

The peace and prosperity most people say they seek isn't in some far off land or in heaven. The Promised Land has already been delivered to you and it is right between your ears. I am a Christian and I believe in eternal life through my Savior, Jesus Christ. I also know that eternal life has already been delivered to me. The words and actions of Jesus do not prepare me for death. *He created a road map for me to LIVE.*

No matter what religion you practice, and no matter what denomination of that religion you engage, you are meant to live. Do you want to live in heaven on earth, or hell on earth? Do you want to wait to get to the Promised Land or do you want to be there now? Do you want to be with your Creator and Savior later, or do you want to be with Them now? The choice is yours.

Be present in the now. Hold your divines in your heart and mind now. Create a life of spiritual and financial well being now. For it is always in the now that we truly live.

WISDOM FOR TODAY:

Date_____

I live my life of abundance now. The Promised Land is always within me.

SCRIPTURE REFERENCE:

"Behold, the kingdom of God is in the midst of you." *Luke 12:21.*

THOUGHTS: _____

_____

_____

_____

_____

_____

_____

_____

_____

_____

ACTIONS: _____

_____

_____

I am fearless™

*A*FFIRMATION:

I Am a consciousness of abundance.

*N*ARRATION:

The word "consciousness" means aware, mindful, alert and having knowledge. When we are mindful or aware of something, it means we are focused on something. If we focus on bills instead of income, what do we attract... more bills. If we are focused on spending instead of investing, what do we do... spend. *When we are focused on wealth, abundance and money, what do we attract... wealth, abundance and money.*

Let's continue on with our definition of "consciousness." When we are alert, we are ready for action. We are ready to accept and act upon the opportunities in life. We are prepared to carry out our intentions and see them through until completion. When we are conscious of abundance, we are ready to create and attract abundance.

"Having knowledge," denotes that we either intuitively or consciously know what to do to create or manifest our abundance. We all know, deep down inside, what our purpose and destiny is in life. We all have dreams, aspirations and goals. We are not asked by God to give those things up for the sake of posterity. We are directed and guided by God to fulfill our destiny for His sake and for ours. Keep in mind that we have an all-knowing and loving God. We do not have a cruel or smite God.

So, exercise your consciousness. Stay aware, mindful and alert. Tap into your intuition and your connection to God; then carry out your destiny with the knowledge and faith that you are doing the right thing.

*W*ISDOM FOR TODAY:

Date_____

I Am aware, mindful and alert to all my opportunities for abundance. I exercise my knowledge and create my destiny as part of God's perfect plan.

*S*CRIPTURE REFERENCE:

"Finally, brethren, whatsoever things are true, whatsoever things are honest, whatsoever things are just, whatsoever things are pure, whatsoever things are lovely, whatsoever things are of good report; if there be any virtue, and if there be any praise, think on these things." *Phillipians 4:8.*

*T*HOUGHTS: _____

_____

_____

_____

_____

_____

_____

_____

*A*CTIONS: _____

_____

I am fearless™

*A*FFIRMATION:

I Am healthy and energetic spiritually, mentally, physically and financially.

*N*ARRATION:

The word healthy also means "whole and sound." The word energetic also means "active, enterprising, vigorous, absolute and perpetual." When we are healthy and energetic spiritually, physically, mentally and financially, we truly are in the spiritual economy. We are divine (I Am), we are whole and sound, and we are actively expressing our abundance. Can you understand why this affirmation is so important? It really is the embodiment of this entire process of truth.

This affirmation describes the necessity of spiritual, mental and physical wholeness to attract financial wealth. *Financial wealth is a spiritual, mental and physical commitment. Our energy in these areas must be true, sound and absolute. When we are enterprising, we are feeding the spiritual economy and we put in motion the energy for perpetual abundance.* Our thoughts and actions are perpetual. They can and do continue to produce results for a very long time, maybe forever. Edison's thoughts and actions illuminated the world. The Wright brothers' thoughts and actions changed the entire world. Einstein's thoughts and actions enlightened generations. I could go on and on. The point is, health and energy, coupled with divine love, are the sources of all supply and abundance. Lack of health and energy creates limitation and desperation.

Ask yourself, "How healthy and energetic am I?" Focus on becoming more healthy and energetic. Accept God's love and divine plan for your life. That is when your fortune will materialize.

*W*ISDOM FOR TODAY:

Date_____

I exercise spiritually, mentally, physically and financially each day. I continually build my health and energy.

*S*CRIPTURE REFERENCE:

"The soul of a lazy man desires, and has nothing; but the soul of the diligent shall be made rich." *Proverbs 13:4.*

*T*HOUGHTS: _____

_____

_____

_____

_____

_____

_____

*A*CTIONS: _____

_____

_____

I am fearless™

AFFIRMATION:

My words are my staff...I declare abundance and I receive abundance.

NARRATION:

The power of the spoken word is described in almost every spiritual writing. Scripture reveals to us many times to "declare" what we desire. How many times have you heard the phrase, "Be careful what you ask for because you will probably get it"? ***The truth is, we always get what we ask for if we are clear in our demands and we have true faith that we shall have it.***

Being clear in our demands seems like such a simple thing doesn't it? You are probably saying to yourself, "I have made my demands clear many times and they haven't materialized." Here is the reason why. Our demands must be made for the right thing, for the right reason, in the right way at the right time. "How do I do that," you ask? This is actually a fairly simple process. If what you declare is part of the natural order of things, and is part of God's divine plan for you at this time, then you shall have it. If it is not part of the divine plan, you may have to exercise some patience. During these times it is important not to carry around resentment or disgust. These emotions just create more lack, limitation and stumbling blocks. During these times we must trust in God and maintain our faith. Do not quit now.

Bear in mind, faith consists of belief in things we cannot see and the courage to continually act prosperously and with an abundance mentality even if our treasure has not materialized yet. Your acts of faith necessitate the eventual outcome. It is already done. Maintain your composure, balance and faith, and what you declare will eventually come to pass.

WISDOM FOR TODAY:

Date_____

I declare a thing and I shall receive it. It is already done. Now I will allow God to deliver what I need for my declaration to materialize at the right time, in the right way for the right reason.

SCRIPTURE REFERENCE:

"Thou shalt decree a thing and it shall be established unto thee: and the light shall shine upon thy ways." *Job 22:28.*

THOUGHTS: _____

_____

_____

_____

_____

_____

_____

_____

ACTIONS: _____

_____

_____

I am fearless™

AFFIRMATION:

I give thanks to God as the source of my abundance. I now accept my financial wealth under grace in a divine way.

NARRATION:

This affirmation expresses the mindset which is essential to developing financial wealth or manifesting any material desire. First, we are giving thanks for what we already have and for what we expect to materialize. Then we declare God as the source of all abundance which He surely is.

We continue on, with specificity, and now declare we accept our financial wealth. Remember, we must have specificity in mind when we make a declaration. Before using this affirmation, have a clear mental picture and number in mind. What does financial wealth mean to you? How does it feel? What does it look like? Is it $20,000, or is it $20,000,000? Is it an income of $100,000 per year, or $100,000 per day? *We each have our own definition of financial wealth. Fix this picture clearly in your mind. Then develop a comfort level with this picture so you do not create anxiety or doubt about its manifestation.*

Finally, we accept its manifestation according to God's divine plan. We also accept it under grace. Keep in mind that a state of grace is a state of total abundance. When we are under grace, there is no lack or limitation, only supply. This is the true environment God has created. There is no loss versus gain, win or lose. There is no karmic law of give and take. There is only supply. God's supply of love and abundance.

WISDOM FOR TODAY:

Date_____

My gratitude, and acceptance of all my desires, now clears the channel for divine manifestation.

SCRIPTURE REFERENCE:

"And now I commend you to God and to the message of His grace, a message that is able to build you up and give you the inheritance among all who are sanctified." *Acts 20:32.*

THOUGHTS: _____

_____

_____

_____

_____

_____

_____

_____

ACTIONS: _____

_____

_____

I am fearless™

ℐFFIRMATION:

God, grant me the right <u>car</u>, extraordinary and fruitful in every way; the one that is part of Your perfect plan.

ℕARRATION:

I have underlined the word car in this affirmation, because you could substitute any other material item in its place. If your desire is for a new home, substitute the word "home" for car. Whatever your material desire is, use this affirmation and fill in your description. But take a look at the underlying meaning of this affirmation. First, you are again acknowledging God as the source of your supply. Then you are staking your claim by describing the item you want to materialize.

Here is where it really gets fun. We stake our claim to something that is "extraordinary and fruitful." We affirm that we are worthy of the best and we are accepting of extraordinary things. We continue with the belief that we want our manifestation to bear fruit as well; that it will continue to produce abundance and the seeds of prosperity—not only for ourselves but for others as well. WOW!

We then go on to claim that we shall accept it as part of God's perfect plan. *We don't want to accept anything that will divert us from the ultimate goal of fulfilling our divine plan.* We declare and receive the perfect house, the perfect car, the perfect relationships, all of which will satisfy us and will be part of the wholeness and completeness of God's perfect plan.

This is a sovereign affirmation. Use it wisely.

WISDOM FOR TODAY:

Date_____

Today, I declare my worthiness of extraordinary relationships and things. My happiness is a sovereign right.

SCRIPTURE REFERENCE:

"Do not worry about anything, but in everything by prayer and supplication with thanksgiving, let your requests be made known to God." *Phillipians 4:6.*

THOUGHTS: _____

_____

_____

_____

_____

_____

_____

_____

ACTIONS: _____

_____

_____

I am fearless™

*A*FFIRMATION:

I have a perfect vision of the divine plan of my life. I see clearly and act faithfully.

*N*ARRATION:

We all think in pictures. We "see" our thoughts because there is a continuous film being created in our minds. We keep impressing pictures on our minds which stay there forever unless we allow them to fade away. We have immediate recall of these pictures both consciously and subconsciously. They can work for us, or we can allow them to work against us. When I state, "Try not to think of twenty dollars," what did your mind do? Of course, you clearly saw a mental picture of twenty dollars.

The amazing thing is that our subconscious doesn't know the difference between real and imaginary pictures. Because we possess this faculty, we can impress any picture we want onto our mental film. The subconscious mind will play the film over and over and will eventually convince the conscious mind this is reality. What a remarkable truth. *Since "seeing is believing," when we physically act upon the pictures that have been playing in our minds, we can manifest them into physical reality.*

The words " I have a perfect vision," are declarative in nature, meaning you declare and expect the divine plan of your life to be revealed to you. Then, you will hold these visions in your mind continuously. And finally, you will create or allow their manifestation. Ask God in His infinite wisdom to deliver your perfect plan. Then visualize it, affirm it and take action. Your dreams will become a reality.

*W*ISDOM FOR TODAY:

The manifestation of all my dreams has begun. The spiritual laws are in motion and I clearly see the picture of my divine plan.

*S*CRIPTURE REFERENCE:

"Lift up now thine eyes, and look from the place where thou art northward, and southward, and eastward, and westward: For all the land which thou seest, to thee I will give it." *Genesis 13:14,15.*

*T*HOUGHTS: _____

_____

_____

_____

_____

_____

_____

_____

_____

*A*CTIONS: _____

_____

_____

I am fearless™

AFFIRMATION:

I Am set free... I release all burdens, doubts and worries.

NARRATION:

So many of us carry burdens, doubts and worries with us, it is no wonder we keep attracting them to ourselves. Set yourself free from these burdens. Most of them were created through our own vain imaginings. We only have two natural fears; the fear of falling and the fear of loud noises. Where did all the rest of them come from?

Each day we can decide to emancipate ourselves from doubt and worry. Through prayer, faith, affirmation, visualization and faithful actions we develop confidence and mental freedom. It is a liberating feeling when we discharge our burdens and doubts. When we cast them off, we return to a natural state of mind. As a result, we also "clear the channels" for wondrous new revelations, ideas, hopes and dreams. All our old burdens and worries are "unnatural" conditions. They have no place in your mind.

Make an inventory of all the worn out conditions, old burdens, self-doubts and worries in your mind. Write them down on a piece of paper to get them "out of your system." Then take a match and burn them. Watch them disappear and your natural self will reappear.

Affirm to yourself, "Today is a day of completion...I Am set free." You will be amazed at the results and the manifestations that will materialize soon thereafter.

WISDOM FOR TODAY:

Date_____

Today is my liberation day. I am emancipated from all doubt, worry, burdens and worn-out conditions. My channels are cleared for my good fortune.

SCRIPTURE REFERENCE:

"Now the Lord is the Spirit, and where the Spirit of the Lord is, there is freedom." *2 Corinthians 3:17.*

THOUGHTS: _____

_____

_____

_____

_____

_____

_____

ACTIONS: _____

_____

_____

_____

I am fearless™

*A*FFIRMATION:

Divine love is perfect love. I Am love in action.

*N*ARRATION:

This is a difficult concept for many people to understand. **When we do all things with love, think with love and accept love, we create a profound ripple effect of love, charity, peace, abundance and prosperity.** Mother Teresa is a phenomenal example of this truth.

There are many quotes attributed to her, but my favorite is, "If you judge someone, you have no time to love them."

Let's take a look at the love, abundance and wealth, including the material and financial wealth, she manifested and continues to manifest even though she has passed on. First, she was always giving her most precious assets to other people with no expectation of anything in return (love, energy and time). She loved what she did. She was (and is) love and charity in action. She created tremendous wealth as well. She created spiritual wealth for the sick, the dying, and for the volunteers and benefactors of her mission. She created mental and emotional wealth through her love-consciousness and her actions. She provided physical health to many. Her thinking was always divine, because, although she was surrounded by illness and perceived limitation, she always thought and acted abundantly.

Here is the amazing point. Although Mother Teresa was "penniless," she created hundreds of millions of dollars of financial wealth. Her donors and benefactors donated mansions, buildings, planes, cars, equipment, medicines, money, advice and services totaling in the millions of dollars. This was not a "poor" woman. This was a rich woman in mind, in heart, in spirit and in action. This is true prosperity and abundance. She cleared the channels with her love, devotion and faithful actions, and the money came.

*W*ISDOM FOR TODAY:

Today, I choose to do what I love and love what I do. When I love what I do and act faithfully, I set the table for total abundance. The money always comes.

*S*CRIPTURE REFERENCE:

"My little children, let us not love in word, neither in tongue; but in deed and in truth." *1 John 3:18.*

*T*HOUGHTS: _____

_____

_____

_____

_____

_____

_____

_____

*A*CTIONS: _____

_____

_____

I am fearless™

AFFIRMATION:

I establish a perfect pattern of truth, abundance and prosperity in my subconscious mind, now and forever.

NARRATION:

Our subconscious minds are the receivers and transmitters of tremendous spiritual and subconscious signals. Our subconscious mind is our direct contact with God (psychologists would call this the Superconscious). *Our subconscious is the gold mind within each one of us. In our subconscious there lies all the answers to every challenge, every hope, and every dream and goal we desire.* If we command our subconscious to deliver us the knowledge we need to carry out our desires, it will do so. But you have to be willing to ask.

How do you establish this perfect pattern of truth, abundance and prosperity? Through prayer, auto-suggestion, affirmation and visualization, you stake your claim to prosperity. You allow God to plant the seeds of abundance (the ideas) in your subconscious and then you act upon them. Whenever we seek an answer from God, we always get it. We may not like the answer, but we get a truthful and all-knowing answer to our prayers. It is up to us to do something with them.

Time after time I have heard people say, "I've been praying so long for the solution to my problems." At some point in time, you must stop praying and start doing. You already have the answer—you already know what you must do. Ask for the perfect plan, the perfect truth and perfect abundance to be delivered to you. It will come, not to your front door, but to your mind. Cultivate and harvest those seeds of perfect abundance and prosperity. Then, riches will come.

*W*ISDOM FOR TODAY:

Date_____

I tap into the power of the all-knowing God through my subconscious mind. My **gold mind** *is stationed within me. I ask. I accept. I act. I complete.*

*S*CRIPTURE REFERENCE:

"God...richly provides us with everything." *1 Timothy 6:17.*

*T*HOUGHTS: _____

_____

_____

_____

_____

_____

_____

_____

*A*CTIONS: _____

_____

_____

_____

I am fearless™

$\mathcal{A}$FFIRMATION:

My income increases freely and easily.

$\mathcal{N}$ARRATION:

This simple affirmation is not simplistic. It is very powerful. If you research the meanings of the words "income", "increases", "freely" and "easily", in a thesaurus or dictionary, you will see what I mean.

The word "income" suggests earnings, profits, wages and receipts. Your income does not have to come from one source, nor should it. When you use this affirmation, you will have the opportunity to increase your income from many sources. It doesn't matter whether you are an employee, self-employed or unemployed. The opportunities will present themselves for you to increase your income—by how much is up to you.

The word "increase" can be defined as growth, expansion or germination. With this affirmation you will find opportunities for personal and financial growth, the opportunity to expand your horizons as well as your income, and this will be done through the germination of the ideas you cultivate into faithful actions.

The word "freely" is described as "without constraint," "without fear," "gratuitously" and "as one pleases." What a summation of this philosophy, all depicted in one word! There is unlimited abundance. When we act faithfully we become fearless spiritually, emotionally and financially. We are always in a state of gratitude, and we are free from all worry and doubt. We become totally free.

The word "easily" denotes effortlessness, absoluteness and lack of doubt. *Things can be easy and come easily if we have the proper mentality. When we trust in God, all things can be done freely and easily.*

*W*ISDOM FOR TODAY:

Date_____

I can accomplish what I want today, easily and effortlessly.
My struggles are over. Abundance is undoubtedly mine.

*S*CRIPTURE REFERENCE:

"I can do everything through Him who gives me strength." *Phillipians 4:13.*

*T*HOUGHTS: _____

_____

_____

_____

_____

_____

_____

_____

*A*CTIONS: _____

_____

_____

_____

I am fearless™

*A*FFIRMATION:

I Am always awake to my opportunities. I act quickly and decisively. I always move through the open door of destiny.

*N*ARRATION:

Do you know someone who always seems to be "getting ready?" Many of us prepare and educate ourselves, but fail to take action when our opportunities come. We tend to get into these stages where we claim we need more information or need more questions answered before we can make a decision. Sometimes this is a valid course of proper preparation and decision making. Many times it is also an excuse not to take a risk or carry through on an opportunity.

Through prayer, visualization, affirmation, and our continual conversations with God, we develop an endless stream of intuitive leads and opportunities. When this happens, we must act quickly and decisively. How many past decisions can you look back upon when you decided not to do something, and you now say to yourself, " I wish I would have...," "I should have..." or "I could have...." The "I should have, could have, would have" syndrome stagnates many people and mandates their mediocrity and poverty for years, sometimes for generations. Keep in mind that mediocrity and poverty are both physical realities and mental realities, the first coming as a result of the latter.

Stop looking through the open door of destiny and walk through it. There is nothing to fear here. Success, abundance, prosperity and wealth are the natural way and the obligatory way. You have a duty to succeed. It is your destiny to succeed. It is your right to succeed.

Your destiny is created in those moments in life when you know what you must do...and then you do it. Do it today!

*W*ISDOM FOR TODAY:

Date_____

Today I give myself permission to succeed. I have no fear of failure or success. My open door of destiny is just before me. I now walk through it.

*S*CRIPTURE REFERENCE:

"I will instruct thee and teach thee in the way which thou shalt go: I will guide thee with mine eye." *Psalm 32:8.*

*T*HOUGHTS: _____

_____

_____

_____

_____

_____

_____

*A*CTIONS: _____

_____

_____

I am fearless™

*A*FFIRMATION:

Perfect good now comes to me in perfect ways.

*N*ARRATION:

This affirmation "re-affirms" your abilities to "draw to yourself" the opportunities and the means to carry out your dreams, goals and desires. We all know by now that there is a perfect plan for our lives, that our opportunities are always right in front of us and our intuition and subconscious always deliver the perfect answers we need from God. Trust that these are the right opportunities and answers, then act on them.

None of us need to be chasing after our dreams. If we develop the right mindset and attitudes, our dreams will chase after us. What a relief! This is what we all *must* do.

1. Pray as a method of giving glory and praise to God and as a method of preparation.
2. Develop a dream list. Get your dreams out of your head and onto paper. This is the first step to manifestation...then develop some short, concise clearly-written goals.
3. Make sure your dreams and goals are congruent with your values and mission (or purpose) in life. Immerse yourself in greatness by attuning or synchronizing yourself in the truth.
4. Visualize and affirm every day. Stake your claim to your dreams and desires.
5. Trust in God and believe the right opportunities will present themselves to you for the fulfillment of your desires (they always do).
6. Give gratitude *now* for the goodness in your life and for the attainment of your dreams and goals, *before they manifest* (some of these affirmations will help you with that).
7. Use your intuition. Carry on a continual conversation with God. Listen for the answers to your prayers and see them. They are all around you, before you, inside of you. Follow where He leads.
8. Accept the answers and take action!!! *Do not prejudge the method, through whom, or the means by which your dreams will manifest.* Be fearless, trust in God's plan, surrender to it; this is the divine plan of your life. Do not wait too long or the opportunity will fade away (and so won't you).
9. Do all things with love. Love what you do and do what you love. Pass on your love through your thoughts, your actions, your work.
10. Accept the manifestation of your dreams and goals (including the money that will follow). Allow them to happen...do not deny them. You deserve to be wealthy and so shall you be.

WISDOM FOR TODAY:

Date_____

I now draw to me my own. There is no necessity to chase after anything or anyone. Success is a natural process and I now carry out the divine plan of my life.

SCRIPTURE REFERENCE:

"Remember to welcome strangers, because some who have done this have welcomed angels without knowing it." *Hebrews 13:2,3.*

THOUGHTS: _____

_____

_____

_____

_____

_____

_____

ACTIONS: _____

_____

_____

I am fearless™

✠FFIRMATION:

I Am free from envy and jealousy...I rejoice in the prosperity of others.

✠ARRATION:

You will notice that several of these affirmations focus on releasing or forgoing envy, resentment and jealousy of others and of what they may have. What we most envy in other people is what we are most lacking ourselves. The more we focus on what we lack, the more of it we draw to ourselves.

For instance, people who have money, riches, abundance and prosperity should be, to some degree, revered. They figured it out. They know how to develop wealth and they either intuitively or consciously follow many, if not all, of the abundance principles. So should you. Do not begrudge anyone their wealth, health or happiness. When you do, you only begrudge yourself and the very process you MUST follow to attain what you are seeking.

Instead, rejoice in the prosperity of others. ***The simple thought that you are happy for the success, wealth and happiness of someone else begins to establish a subconscious acceptance of an abundant life.*** Share in the wealth of others. Learn from them. Become conscious of wealth. As often as possible, immerse yourself in wealthy thoughts, actions and environments. Get comfortable with the feeling of wealth. Until you are comfortable with wealth, you will not have it.

WISDOM FOR TODAY:

Date_____

I rejoice in the wealth and prosperity of others. I seek to find wealthy environments so I may develop comfort and peace with wealth.

SCRIPTURE REFERENCE:

"As we have therefore opportunity, let us do good unto all men, especially unto them who are of the right household of faith." *Galatians 6:10.*

THOUGHTS: _____

_____

_____

_____

_____

_____

_____

_____

ACTIONS: _____

_____

_____

I am fearless™

*A*FFIRMATION:

By day and by night, I Am flourishing in all of my interests.

*N*ARRATION:

Wealth, abundance, prosperity and money don't stop working at 5:00PM; neither should your prosperous mentality. God doesn't sleep when we do, nor does our subconscious mind. They are both allies, working, producing, delivering and protecting, 24 hours a day. Prosperity thinking cannot stop simply because you are preparing for sleep. As a matter of fact, this is a prime time for your prosperity thinking to produce results.

Your thoughts are always producing results. Your mind, your prayers, your visions, your spoken words, are always in action. What an astonishing truth. Developing wealth, money and material desires, passing on our love, and carrying out the divine plan of our lives, is not a 9am to 5pm job. It is a 24-hour, natural and fruitful, way of life.

This affirmation can make a significant difference in your life. It is an attestation of the natural emanation of abundance. There is no conflict here, only an inherent manifestation of God's truth....that is...wealth, abundance and prosperity are the genuine and honest path intended for all of us. We don't need to make life hard, we don't need to fail in order to succeed. We don't need to invoke pain in order to find pleasure and we don't need to experience scarcity to appreciate prosperity.

We simply need to make up our minds that we deserve it and then surrender to and accept abundance as the natural way for us.

WISDOM FOR TODAY:

Date_____

Prosperity is my way of life. My abundant thoughts and actions are always working in my favor. I accept prosperity as the right path for me.

SCRIPTURE REFERENCE:

"For whatever is born of God overcomes the world..." *1 John 5:4.*

THOUGHTS: _____

_____

_____

_____

_____

_____

_____

_____

_____

ACTIONS: _____

_____

_____

I am fearless™

*A*FFIRMATION:

Money circulates freely in my life. The channels of wealth are always open.

*N*ARRATION:

Money, like other forms of energy, can flow freely or experience blockages. Money flows freely into and through our lives because of our attitudes and beliefs. The same holds true for the times we are lacking money. The blockage of the natural flow of money into and through our lives is not a result of the economy, the Federal Reserve, or interest rates. If we lack money, it is because we have lost touch with the spiritual economy. For example, the years in which I have earned the most money, have been years when the economy has been at its worst. This is because I do not accept the notion that the government, banks or other forces dictate my abundance. My thoughts, beliefs, actions and faith do.

The same holds true for you. To whom are you faithful? To whom are you loyal? Shakespeare said it well, "To thine own self be true." Shakespeare's reference was to be true to your thoughts, your faith and your intuition. Don't surrender your thoughts to anyone but God. If you are not in control of your own subconscious mind, somebody else is. If you allow negative thinking, faithless thinking, the attitudes and beliefs of others to determine your worth, they will also determine your wealth.

Money reacts the same way. The stock market was down 200 points yesterday. So WHAT! Yesterday, I established a business relationship that will produce hundreds of thousands of dollars for me and my family for generations. *There is no connection between the wealth you may have and the regular economy. The connection is between you, God, the love you have for others and for what you do, the willingness to accept your naturally available prosperity, and your conviction in staking your claim to it. This is the spiritual economy.*

Don't be fooled by the economists. The only limitation to your wealth lies within you.

Make up your mind to allow money to flow and circulate in your life all the time. You are always an open channel for wealth.

*W*ISDOM FOR TODAY:

Date_____

I Am always in control of my financial destiny. The door is always open to my good and no man can shut it.

*S*CRIPTURE REFERENCE:

"Blessed is the man who walks not in the counsel of the wicked, nor stands in the way of the sinners, nor sits in the seat of scoffers; but his delight is in the law of the Lord, and on his law he meditates day and night, He is like a tree planted by steams of water, that yields its fruit in season and its leaf does not wither. In all that he does he prospers." *Psalms 1:1-3.*

*T*HOUGHTS: _____

_____

_____

_____

_____

_____

_____

_____

*A*CTIONS: _____

_____

I am fearless™

𝒜FFIRMATION:

*I Am passionate about my **business**. I love what I do and I do it often.*

𝒩ARRATION:

In this affirmation, I have underscored the word "business." I have a great passion and love for our business interests. You can replace the word "business" with "career", "profession," "vocation," "calling," or something similar. I personally abhor the word "job." This word proclaims boredom, lack of excitement and routine. A "profession" is exciting and progressive.

This affirmation makes you stop, think about and respond to the questions, "Do I love what I do?" and "Do I really have a passion for what I do?" If you can't answer "yes" to both of these questions, than why are you doing it? You can "earn a living" doing anything. If you have made up your mind to "earn a living," at least do so at something you love to do. I have heard every excuse in the book about this one. "I can't make enough money doing what I would really love to do," "It's too late for me to change now," and "I have to support my family" are the most common excuses. You can make more than enough money doing anything if you really love it, are committed to it, and follow God's plan for the manifestation of your desires. I know "junk" dealers who "make" more money than lawyers and doctors. I know teachers who "make" more money than stockbrokers. *Money doesn't come as a result of what you do; it comes as a result of who you are and the faith you exhibit in your beliefs.*

Make a choice to do what you love. Be creative about how you do it. Write some dreams and goals on how you can and should accomplish this. Use the manifestation process described in this book and make a *transition* to doing what you love to do. Gather the support of your loved ones and explain why this is important to everyone. Then do it.

You were born to live, not just survive. Forget about the metaphysical explanations you may have heard... that you are just experiencing what you must experience right now to nourish your soul. You are where you are right now because of your choices or lack thereof, your faith or your lack thereof, your fearlessness or your fearfulness. Make a choice to live and glorify God with your unique gifts and talents. Put them to use for your sake and for His. Do this with love and out of love. The money will follow.

WISDOM FOR TODAY:

Date_____

Today, I make up my mind to do what I love and love what I do. I make a plan for the transition to life and career of passion.

SCRIPTURE REFERENCE:

"Wherefore the rather, brethren, give diligence to make your calling and election sure: for if ye do these things, you shall never fall." *2 Peter 1:10.*

THOUGHTS: _____

_____

_____

_____

_____

_____

_____

_____

ACTIONS: _____

_____

_____

I am fearless™

$\mathscr{A}$FFIRMATION:

I give thanks to God as the wellspring of my supply. I now create and accept **the hundreds of thousands of dollars** *that come to me easily and abundantly through* **book and tape sales, speaking engagements and personal coaching.**

$\mathscr{N}$ARRATION:

This is a good example of the "spoken word", "gratitude", "visualization", "acceptance" and "synchronization" aspects of manifesting wealth. Again, several words have been underscored. This is my affirmation. You may want to replace the words "hundreds of thousands of dollars" to "thousands of dollars or millions of dollars." If you are going to manifest your wealth through a specific business or profession, you will change the words "book and tape sales, speaking engagements and personal coaching" to your chosen business or career.

But let's take a look at what we have done with this affirmation. First of all, we have acknowledged God as the wellspring of our abundance and we are giving gratitude for our expected manifestation. We have staked our claim to our good. We have exercised our claim through this affirmation with both the written and spoken word, and we can clearly "see" the actions, and results of the actions, we are about to take. We can see the money "piling up" before us, and we can see ourselves rendering the service(s) we love to render. We also display our willingness to accept abundance and money because we have specified money, and we are synchronizing our love for what we do, with God and with the manifestation of money.

Use the format of this affirmation for the manifestation of your wealth, your supply. *Decree a thing and it shall be yours.*

WISDOM FOR TODAY:

Date_____

When I decree a thing, I shall have positive expectations for its manifestation. I have these expectations because I faithfully take action and follow the divine plan to manifest that which I declared to be mine.

SCRIPTURE REFERENCE:

"A man hath joy by the answer of his mouth: and a word spoken in season, how good is it!" *Proverbs 15:23.*

THOUGHTS: _____

_____

_____

_____

_____

_____

_____

_____

ACTIONS: _____

_____

_____

I am fearless™

*A*FFIRMATION:

All my goals, or something better, are now manifesting for me in totally gratifying and plentiful ways.

*N*ARRATION:

In order for this affirmation to work, you must have some goals and they must be in writing. For a more extensive narration of the necessity of goal setting, refer to my book, *Affirmations of Wealth – 101 Secrets of Daily Success.* Goal setting and committing our dreams and goals to writing is crucial to our success and to the manifestation of our dreams, goals, money and material desires. *Even more crucial, however, is to not become so focused on "how" we perceive the goal should be accomplished that we miss out on the opportunities to accomplish our goals. Remember, we are seeking to synchronize with God's plan, the divine plan. We are seeking a specific result, not necessarily the specific path we must take to get there.*

Here is a real life example of this concept. When I first published *Affirmations of Wealth,* I had a goal to be an internationally recognized author and motivational speaker. I affirmed over and over, "I Am an internationally recognized best-selling author and motivational speaker." My perception was that I would find a publisher, get the book published, and then, through marketing and public relations, my dream would be fulfilled. Next, I would be a guest on radio and television programs and my notoriety would propel my speaking and writing career! Well, I was wrong.

What actually happened? As a result of publishing *Affirmations of Wealth,* I was contacted by several local representatives for different network marketing organizations (also commonly referred to as multi-level marketing companies), all of whom wanted my wife and I to join their organizations. At first, I was closed-minded to the idea, but I was open enough to listen to the opportunities. As a result, we did associate with a wonderful network marketing company (there are many), and we have sold thousands of books, and performed seminars for thousands of people in this company and others—all over the country and soon all over the world. But here is the amazing part: we have developed an additional income stream from our network marketing business that will total in the millions of dollars during our lifetime and much more thereafter. If I had stayed tied to my perception, instead of allowing God to help me see the divine plan of my life, I would have missed the tremendous wealth, success, happiness, abundance, love and friendships that we now have. Put your ego aside for a moment and let God do His work. If He has "something better" in mind, a more perfect means to the end result, do it.

WISDOM FOR TODAY:

Date_____

I aim for my goals but I keep an open mind on how to get there. Sometimes, with God's help, there is a better way. I ask for the answers and at times they come in a surprising way.

SCRIPTURE REFERENCE:

"Strive for the greater gifts. And I will show you a still more excellent way."
1 Corinthians 12:31.

THOUGHTS: _____

_____

_____

_____

_____

_____

_____

_____

ACTIONS: _____

_____

_____

I am fearless™

AFFIRMATION:

My financial success is now assured. Money comes to me easily and effortlessly.

NARRATION:

Financial success, and accepting the full abundance of the spiritual economy, is not something that has to wait. Your financial success can begin to manifest today. The word "assured" means undoubted, guaranteed and sure. Your financial success is undoubted, guaranteed and sure, if you are. Your guarantee has already come in a promise from God. With such a guarantee, how could you have any doubts or insecurities about your financial abundance?

Please, please, please, continue to keep in mind that the manifestation of financial freedom is not a secret—it is a process. The only secrets about financial freedom are the secrets we harbor ourselves. Financial freedom, and the natural demonstration thereof, can be as easy as the making of a free-throw by Michael Jordan, the writing of a poem by Emily Dickinson, or the making of a movie by Steven Spielberg. These are all natural occurrences, full of creative energy, performed as an expression of love, delivered in their truest forms, seemingly effortless and pure in their intention. And so is the attraction of money, the earning of money, the circulation of money and the proliferation of money.

Creating, accepting and manifesting wealth, must, and will, be a natural process for you. Make money a natural part of your life. Respect it, appreciate it, accept it with love and circulate it with love, give it your blessings, your dreams, your goodness and it will do the same for you.

*W*ISDOM FOR TODAY:

Date_____

Money is now a natural part of my life. I treat it with respect and love and it does the same for me.

*S*CRIPTURE REFERENCE:

"Therefore I do not run uncertainty (without definite aim)..." *1 Corinthians 9:26.*

*T*HOUGHTS: _____

_____

_____

_____

_____

_____

_____

_____

*A*CTIONS: _____

_____

_____

I am fearless™

AFFIRMATION:

Every day I Am growing more financially free. I Am rich, I Am wealthy, I Am happy.

NARRATION:

For many of us, attaining financial freedom is a maturation process. As we continue to grow and mature in our lives, we begin to understand the truth about ourselves and the value of money. Our responsibility is to continue to grow ourselves and to continue to grow our money. Many of us refuse to be responsible with money because we don't want to be responsible for ourselves, our thoughts, our actions or our inaction.

Enlightenment is a foundation of financial freedom. When we become enlightened to the truth about our lives, assume responsibility, and follow the intended path for us, we mature into financial freedom. This affirmation confirms financial freedom as a process. I specifically used the word "growing" to invoke thoughts of continual evolution and advancement. If we stagnate personally, we stagnate financially. If we stagnate spiritually, we stagnate financially. The spiritual economy abhors a vacuum. Stagnation is contrary to the laws of nature and the laws of money.

As we grow in our enlightenment, assume responsibility for our words, our thoughts, our actions and our relationship with God, we also open the channels to grow in financial freedom. Have the courage to do a true inventory of your personal and financial situation. There is a checklist in this book to help you do this. Be honest. Then decide to accept the responsibility for your present and future happiness. God will be your guide if you allow Him to be. Riches, wealth and happiness are the natural path. Leave the old worn out conditions behind and begin to grow into your financial freedom.

WISDOM FOR TODAY:

Date_____

Today, I assume responsibility for the condition of my life. I learn from my past experiences and I let the rest go. I Am on the path to financial freedom.

SCRIPTURE REFERENCE:

"Behold, I will do a new thing: now it shall spring forth; shall ye not know it? I will even make a way in the wilderness, and rivers in the desert." *Isaiah 43:19.*

THOUGHTS: _____

_____

_____

_____

_____

_____

_____

_____

ACTIONS: _____

_____

_____

I am fearless™

*A*FFIRMATION:

All the wealth and money I have ever desired now manifests before my eyes under grace in a perfect way.

*N*ARRATION:

Do you believe that all things are possible? Jesus did. Mother Teresa did. The Prophets did. The Apostles did. Why shouldn't you? *In many regards, the realization of financial freedom, and the manifestation of material desires, is simply an extension of faith.* What are the components of faith? They are: belief in what cannot be immediately seen, love, trust, expectations, conviction, fidelity, humility and acceptance. You can add your own description of faith in the notes section on the next page. *The point is, what we believe about faith, and how we demonstrate faith through our actions, is consistent with how close we are to financial, time, material and emotional freedom.*

Do you believe financial freedom is possible for you? Do you really believe this? Do you believe you deserve this? Do you believe you shall have this? If so, how are you going to demonstrate your faith for the manifestation of your financial freedom? What is your next faithful action going to be? These are the questions that must be answered. Look at all the examples given above: Jesus, Mother Teresa, the Prophets, the Apostles. Did they just sit around and hope their missions would be accomplished, or did they go out and do something about it? They asked God to reveal His purpose for them...He did. They asked God for the courage to carry out their purpose...He gave it to them. They gave, received and did all things with love. They asked God for the means, the direction and the signs to follow...He provided them. They sought the truth, had faith in what they could not see, had complete trust in Him, fulfilled their expectations with conviction, remained loyal to their cause, to themselves and to God, and accepted their calling with humility and grace. They took action...and so did God.

You have the same power within you. You can accept the same responsibility and manifest your dreams. This is not a complicated matter...it is simply a matter of faith.

WISDOM FOR TODAY:

Date_____

I believe in God and in myself. Through my faithful actions I shall now manifest my personal and financial destiny.

SCRIPTURE REFERENCE:

"All things are possible to him who believes." *Mark 9:23.*

THOUGHTS: _____

_____

_____

_____

_____

_____

_____

ACTIONS: _____

_____

_____

I am fearless™

AFFIRMATION:

I Am now open to receiving all the wondrous blessings of this abundant world. Hundreds of thousands of dollars now flow in under grace in a perfect way.

NARRATION:

There are many lessons in this affirmation, but for now we are going to focus on the money. Let's look at the underscored section of the affirmation. The words "hundreds of thousands" are underscored. You can fill in any dollar amount your mind will accept here. *Our minds, to some degree, are also creatures of habit.* If you immediately write this affirmation and fill in the words "millions of dollars," the affirmation will only work if it is not in conflict with your subconscious beliefs. This is the major mistake most people make with affirmations. We cannot create conflicts in our own minds and expect the manifestation of our affirmations. If you are used to dealing with "millions" of dollars, then go ahead and use the word "millions." But if you now earn $30,000 per year, and you are paid in $600 increments, your mind cannot understand the concept of "millions" of dollars. Use dollar amounts or descriptions that you can accept, then work your way up.

At one point in time, if I used the term "hundreds of thousands" of dollars, my underlying reaction would have been, "Sure buddy...get a life...this isn't coming to you." Now, I am comfortable and I can understand the concept of "hundreds of thousands" of dollars, and so can my conscious and subconscious minds. So you may want to start with the words "hundreds" or "thousands" or "tens of thousands" first, because this is easy for you to conceptualize. After attaining these levels of increased income and wealth, raise the bar and make the faithful leap to the next level.

You can easily achieve and attain what you can "see" and what you can "feel." You can also achieve anything that is not in conflict with your beliefs or experiences. For now, unless you do have a substantial income and material wealth, choose an affirmation that will build up your experience with money. Create more money and wealth incrementally. When you are ready for the big leagues, increase your demands and expectations and you shall have them as well.

WISDOM FOR TODAY:

Date_____

Although I believe all things are possible, I know I must train my mind to accept this truth. I do so by winning small victories every day. Then winning, accepting and receiving shall become an exciting, but common, way of life for me.

SCRIPTURE REFERENCE:

"And let us not grow weary while doing good work, for in due season we shall reap if we do not lose heart." *Galatians 6:9.*

THOUGHTS: _____

_____

_____

_____

_____

_____

_____

_____

ACTIONS: _____

_____

_____

I am fearless™

AFFIRMATION:

I appreciate the value of time and the time-value of money.

NARRATION:

If you respect time, time respects you. If you respect money, money respects you. Simple statements but not simplistic results. Time and money are two things we all say we want more of but seem to be lacking. I keep hearing statements from people who attend my seminars such as, "If I only had more time," or "I don't have enough time," or "There isn't enough time." The same declarations are made about money or the lack thereof: "If I only had more money," "I don't have enough money," etc. By now you should be completely aware of the power of the spoken word; we get what we declare and what we act upon. If you are always declaring the lack of time and money, what do you think you will continually create? More lack of time and money, of course.

Everyone has the same amount of time, yet some people seem to have so much more of it and seem to enjoy their time so much more. This is true because they respect and appreciate time and they are true to their commitments. Time is one of the most precious and productive assets we have. It cannot be wasted. According to metaphysicians, time is constant and infinite. Ask someone who is 80 whether they think that theory is true. We are dealing with reality here. *Time may be infinite, but our ability to conceptualize and use time isn't. We either prioritize and utilize our time properly, or in the real sense, we lose and waste it.* The same holds true for money. We can respect it, accept it and properly utilize it, or we can lose and waste it.

Make up your mind to respect and appreciate time and money. The more you respect and appreciate them, the more you will have.

WISDOM FOR TODAY:

Date_____

Today, I learn how to use a time management system. I prioritize and schedule my time for my maximum benefit. When I respect time, there is plenty for me to accomplish my goals.

SCRIPTURE REFERENCE:

"Therefore be careful how you walk, not as unwise men, but as wise, making most of your time..." *Ephesians 5:15,16.*

THOUGHTS: _____

_____

_____

_____

_____

_____

_____

_____

ACTIONS: _____

_____

_____

I am fearless™

$\mathcal{A}$FFIRMATION:

I invest my time wisely and it produces marvelous returns.

$\mathcal{N}$ARRATION:

Continuing on with the value of time and the time-value of money, in a very real sense, time is money. ***When we properly earn, circulate, save and invest money, time helps us produce incredible results.*** Time can work for us or against us; we can work with it or against it.

The prevalent mindset for many people is, "someday I am going to...." If you want more time and money now, then *now is the time.* Look at any compound interest chart. For each year you don't save or invest your money, you lose thousands of dollars over the life of the investment or during your lifetime. $1,000 invested at 10% each year for 30 years is exponentially greater than $1,000 invested at 10% each year for 20 years. For another example, take a look at a mortgage payment schedule. Paying off your mortgage over 20 years instead of 30 years saves you thousands and thousands of dollars.

So there is a direct correlation between time and the creation of money, as well as how we use our time and the creation of money. If I invested my time to play golf instead of writing this book, the reality is I would have had fun playing golf, but I would have missed the incredible personal, social, spiritual and financial gains from writing this book. Because I invested my time properly, the return on my investment is exponential. And now, as a result of the proper investment of my time, I can play golf wherever and whenever I want.

You have to make the same choices every day. Should I do this...or that? When making your decisions from this point on, keep in mind that time is an indispensable asset. In a very true sense...time is money. Make your decisions on spending or investing time, the same way you make decisions on spending or investing money. Use it to your advantage. Spend, save, donate and invest it responsibly.

WISDOM FOR TODAY:

Date_____

The rules of time are the same as the rules of investing. Today, I gain an exponential return on my investment of time.

SCRIPTURE REFERENCE:

"Remember how short my time is..." *Psalm 89:47.*

THOUGHTS: _____

_____

_____

_____

_____

_____

_____

_____

ACTIONS: _____

_____

_____

_____

I am fearless™

AFFIRMATION:

All my investments are profitable.

NARRATION:

Every day we make spiritual, family, financial, mental, social and physical investments. A spiritual investment may come in the form of allowing yourself time for prayer, giving gratitude, or serving others. A family investment may come in the form of telling your husband/wife and children that you love them, having a meal together, or going shopping with your mom. There are multitudes of financial investments, including where we focus and how we prioritize our time. There are investment accounts, mutual funds, stocks, and all kinds of financial investments. Mental investments are such things as reading books, listening to tapes, attending seminars, meditating, and all forms of preparing or enhancing our mental health. Social investments are made by enhancing our communities with gifts of time, money and expertise. Physical investments can be in the form of proper sleeping habits, exercise, stress reduction, and maintaining a healthy diet. You can describe your own "investments," and the returns you are receiving on these investments, in the Financial Self-Discovery Checklist section.

When making these investments, be very conscious of their power. Expect a positive return on all that you do. Prior to investing time, energy and love on any endeavor or in any relationship, ask yourself: "Is this a good investment? Why am I making this investment? Is this part of my mission? Is this investment harmonious with my values?" Invest in every aspect of your life so you will be whole and fulfilled. All your investments will be profitable when you are faithful to your divine plan, you faithfully carry out your mission, you do all things with love, you invest in God's principles, and your investments are harmonious with your values.

WISDOM FOR TODAY:

Date_____

I invest love, energy and time in every aspect of my life. I Am whole and I Am profitable in every way.

SCRIPTURE REFERENCE:

"And whatever you do, do it heartily, as to the Lord and not to men."
Colossians 3:23.

THOUGHTS: _____

_____

_____

_____

_____

_____

_____

ACTIONS: _____

_____

_____

I am fearless™

*A*FFIRMATION:

My accounts are abundant and overflowing.

*N*ARRATION:

We keep all types of "accounts" in our lives and in our minds. We have spiritual, emotional and financial "bank accounts" that travel with us everywhere we go. I urge you to start thinking of every account as an investment account—one that will bring marvelous returns. I also urge you to close the accounts that are no longer needed or are no longer producing results. These accounts may consist of bad relationships, investments that need to be liquidated because they are not bearing fruit, or old thoughts and paradigms that prevent you from advancing in life.

As an important subconscious exercise, you must also "rename" your accounts. For example, the word "savings" account denotes a measure of desperation. It mandates that we should run to the bank to "save" ourselves by withdrawing money. Change the name of your savings account to "investment" account. Literally get out your passbook or monthly statement and write the words investment account on it. If you track your accounts on a computer, change the word from savings to investment. This may sound somewhat inconsequential, but to your subconscious this is a very important distinction.

Keep going. Rename your Individual Retirement Account. What does the word retire rhyme with?...the word expire. This is an account for living life to its fullest, not to pay for your expiration. Call this your "I Am" account. The very initials IRA give one a negative feeling because they remind us of IRS. Change them to IAM. Reaffirm your abundance every time you deposit or invest in this account by affirming the words, I Am. How about your checking account? The very word "check" means stop, barrier or obstacle. Change the name of this account to the "benefit " account. The word "benefit" is described in the dictionary as "for a worthy cause, gain or advantage." Our subconscious interprets these subtle messages and delivers their intentions to us. Be careful how you phrase the name of your accounts. These are examples only. Be creative, have fun. Your accounts will be overflowing.

WISDOM FOR TODAY:

Date_____

Today, I review my accounts and do a complete and honest inventory. I release what I no longer need. I "rename" my accounts so they may bring me greater abundance.

SCRIPTURE REFERENCE:

"...but this one thing I do: forgetting what lies behind and straining forward to what lies ahead, I press on toward the goal." *Phillipians 3:13,14.*

THOUGHTS: _____

_____

_____

_____

_____

_____

_____

_____

ACTIONS: _____

_____

_____

I am fearless™

*A*FFIRMATION:

I now release all debts of the past. I Am completely debt free.

*N*ARRATION:

Our financial debts are an extension of our psychic, emotional, familiar or spiritual debts. How we feel about ourselves can determine our debt level. Guilt, low self-esteem and selfishness all lead to the manifestation of financial debt. How we observed our parents "spending" and incurring debt has a direct bearing on what we now emotionally and physically do. Our subconscious minds are incredibly fine tuned and they believe whatever we tell them.

Just think about this one example for a moment. You probably have a piece (or several pieces) of plastic that are commonly referred to as credit cards. The very word is an oxymoron. When we look at the true definition of the word "credit" it means trust, credibility, power or merit. The financial institutions and other vendors who issue these cards are in effect saying, "We trust you." Or are they? They are really saying we trust you if you pay us 13% to 21% interest. This is not a credit card. It is a debt card.

It is no wonder the majority of people who use credit (debt) cards never pay them off. This is another way to satisfy our subconscious desires or feelings of guilt, selfishness and low self-esteem, or to continue the financial and emotional patterns of our family. Our minds are so creative. They may deliver the message, "If we don't incur debt the way the rest of our family did, then we are being disloyal to our heritage." Someone must break the chain of emotional and financial debt. That someone is you. ***There is only one responsible way to use a credit (debt) card. You must already have the money set aside to pay for the debt when you receive the notice of payment due. If you cannot do this 100% of the time, cut your credit (debt) cards in half and dispose of them.*** Forget about "trying to cover them" when the bill comes in. The bill is already in at the moment you make the decision to use the card.

The most effective way to lower or release debt is to stop spending, build or rebuild your self-esteem, and distinguish your emotional problems—including guilt. Release your debt familiarity with the past. Decide to live free and so shall you be.

*W*ISDOM FOR TODAY:

Date _____

I have the courage and wisdom to release my debts without losing my identity. I Am forever conscious of my true worth. I now create a legacy of good fortune and abundance.

*S*CRIPTURE REFERENCE:

"Don't let the world around you squeeze you into its own mold, but let God remold your mind from within." *Romans 12:2.*

*T*HOUGHTS: _____

_____

_____

_____

_____

_____

_____

_____

*A*CTIONS: _____

_____

_____

_____

I am fearless™

AFFIRMATION:

I now create a legacy of financial abundance, prosperity and joy.

NARRATION:

Our "familiarity," or our heritage, can and does play a role in our financial and personal wealth. It is no wonder that families whose customary lifestyle includes wealth, abundance and money, usually have children that follow the same pattern. *Our familiarity with money can, and in most cases does, get passed down from generation to generation. The word "familiar" is defined as customary, usual or well known. The root of the word (family) means lineage or ancestry. In simple terms, this means we pass on our traits to our children and other family members.*

If you have a family heritage rich in abundance and prosperity, most likely you will continue that legacy. If you have a family heritage of debt, lack or loss, you most likely will carry on that legacy as well. But once you become aware of the thinking that may be holding you back, you can change it. A very common pattern that I have seen, are people who want to be financially and personally successful, but always seem to fall just short. They can't figure out why all the hard work, prayers, affirmations and dedication to their plan isn't working, or continually gets sabotaged. Here is the answer. If you subconsciously or consciously feel like you are disloyal to your heritage of debt, lack or loss, than you are being disloyal to your bloodline. Many of us have a hard time believing this is true, but it is. Consciously we strive for success, we do the right things, but some how, some way, we fall short. This is not because of a lack of will, a lack of desire or a lack of wanting to do the right thing; it is simply an innate human tendency.

Do an inventory of your familiarity with money, success and wealth. Can you see or feel any roadblocks, traits or thoughts that may be in your way? Accept them as part of your heritage, but put them aside. Do not ignore them, just don't apply them. Decide that you are going to create the legacy that is right for you and your family. Be conscious of your familiar patterns. Bring along the good and let the rest go.

𝒲ISDOM FOR TODAY:

Date_____

I can create a legacy of abundance for generations to come. I accept the good from my past and I let the rest go without guilt or worry. My heritage is now rich and forever will be.

𝒮CRIPTURE REFERENCE:

" I have set before you life and death, the blessings and the curses; therefore choose life, that you and your descendants may live." *Deuteronomy 30:19.*

𝒯HOUGHTS: _____

_____

_____

_____

_____

_____

_____

_____

𝒜CTIONS: _____

_____

_____

_____

I am fearless™

AFFIRMATION:

I Am forever conscious of my true worth.

NARRATION:

So much in life (and I suspect in eternal life as well) depends on what we think. Being conscious means to be aware, have purpose and to have intention. When we are conscious of our thoughts, the laws of nature dictate that we can also predict the results of our thoughts. When we are consciously thinking about abundance and prosperity, probability demands that is what we will receive. Here is an important revelation...*there are no idle thoughts! Every thought we think produces results. Every thought we think is eternal (until it is unthought). And every thought we think expands.*

If you have thoughts of unworthiness, your subconscious accepts it as the truth, acts on it, expands it and returns an unworthy result. The great news is the opposite is also true. If we have thoughts of worthiness, our subconscious accepts it as truth, acts upon it and returns a worthy result. Where many of us run into trouble is that we haven't weeded out all the old thoughts that are still producing negative results. **Unthink them.** How do you unthink them? Be creative. I write down all my negative beliefs, emotions and thoughts on a piece of paper, and then I burn them up. Sometimes I visualize them in a junk heap that soon disappears. Use whatever method seems right for you, but for God's sake, do it.

Then replace your old discarded thoughts with new ones. Give yourself new images of wealth, riches, money, abundance, happiness, whatever you desire. **Think and act on these things** and you will be conscious, intentional and purposeful in the creation and proliferation of your wealth.

This affirmation, and the content of this affirmation, is very important to your financial wealth. Use this affirmation often. Keep thinking the thoughts that will produce and expand your riches.

*W*ISDOM FOR TODAY:

I Am worthy of success and financial riches. I think worthy thoughts and I produce worthy results.

*S*CRIPTURE REFERENCE:

"Do not be hasty in word or impulsive thought to bring up a matter in the presence of God." *Ecclesiastes 5:2.*

*T*HOUGHTS: _____

_____

_____

_____

_____

_____

_____

_____

*A*CTIONS: _____

_____

_____

I am fearless™

AFFIRMATION:

The foundation of my financial house is strong and permanent.

NARRATION:

This affirmation allows us to have a clear mental picture and understanding of financial wealth. What are the foundations of financial wealth? God, Truth, Gratitude, The Spoken Word, Faith, Love, Purpose (following the Divine Plan) and Acceptance.

These are the building blocks to your financial success. Money mastery is directly related to personal mastery. Freedom from mental slavery directly leads to financial freedom. How are you going to build your financial house? What is it going to look like? When will it materialize? It is time to set some goals.

Setting financial goals can be fun and easy. I recommend that you set a yearly goal in the following areas; income, near term investments (savings), circulation (spending, giving, donating), I Am or financial independence (retirement), and long term investments (making more money with your money). You can add others if you wish, but these should be the basics. These five accounts clearly define the purpose and intent of the money to be deposited into each. *Create a budget* and stick with it. Monitor your goals monthly.

Here is a piece of advice I strongly urge you to accept and follow. *Do not use your checking account as your main deposit account or as your savings account.* Think about this logically for a moment. When money goes into a checking account, your intent and the intent of the money, *is to be spent.* It is too easy to spend money when it is "just sitting there" waiting to be spent. Use your (savings) near term investment account as your main account. Transfer money to your checking account *only* when it is time to pay bills. If you have direct deposit for your pay, have it direct deposited to your savings account, not your checking account. This will force you to *think before you spend.*

*W*ISDOM FOR TODAY:

Today I set clear goals for earning, saving, investing and spending money. My financial future is assured because I have set the proper foundation.

*S*CRIPTURE REFERENCE:

"Go up to the hills and bring wood and build a house." *Haggai 1:8.*

*T*HOUGHTS: _____

_____

_____

_____

_____

_____

_____

_____

*A*CTIONS: _____

_____

_____

I am fearless™

*A*FFIRMATION:

I Am value(s) centered in all my investments.

*N*ARRATION:

Here is a fundamental truth for all investing. You must invest in companies which most closely reflect your personal values. When you invest in a company (through stocks, bonds, mutual funds, etc.), you pass on your energy to that company. You should only pass on your energy to companies that understand, accept and reflect your values, purpose and intent. People who invest to make a "quick few bucks" off the latest hot stock, may inadvertently be investing in a company, or a value system, that is not harmonious with themselves or their goals. These investors make a "few bucks" and then they "take their profits." Well, when investors take their profits, they may also take the negative and unprincipled energy from that company as well. Inevitably, when this happens, the profits that were taken short-term are either immediately reinvested in an investment that loses, are spent frivolously, or are used disingenuously.

Here are some guidelines for investing: 1. Do some homework first. Find out the true nature of the company's products and services. Find out who is running the company, what their values are, and if they have a track record of prosperity thinking and wealth building. 2. Invest in what you know the most about. If you are a nurse, you may want to invest in a principle centered health insurance company, a medical center or a medical supply company. You know the products, you use them every day. If you are a computer technician you may want to invest in a principle centered computer hardware maker. You work with the components every day. 3. Never invest if you are not feeling well spiritually, emotionally or physically. Your spiritual, emotional or physical illness will most likely lead to financial illness. 4. Invest for the long term. Short-term thinking leads to short-term results. If you are in the investment market for a "quick hit.," you may get one. 5. Choose a financial advisor who has an abundance mentality and is most compatible with your individual values and principles. 6. Pray, affirm and visualize your financial success. Pass on your blessings and gratitude for success to the management of the companies you invest in.

*W*ISDOM FOR TODAY:

Date_____

I pass on my energy, through my investments, to companies that are deserving of such. I invest with principles, not with emotions.

*S*CRIPTURE REFERENCE:

"Let me be weighed on honest scales, that God may know my integrity." *Job 31:6.*

*T*HOUGHTS: _____

_____

_____

_____

_____

_____

_____

*A*CTIONS: _____

_____

_____

_____

I am fearless™

AFFIRMATION:

I bank on my success.

NARRATION:

Choosing a financial institution can be fun. Keep in mind, the solvency and success of your bank is a reflection of the solvency and success of its directors, management, employees and customers. Have you ever walked into a bank or financial institution and gotten an instant or gut feeling of success and prosperity or, to the contrary, coldness and indifference? The feeling you get when you go into an environment, like a bank, is probably a fairly accurate indication of whether this is the right bank for you.

Remember the banking crisis of the 1980's and early 1990's. Most of those banks failed as a result of greed, envy, jealousy and ego. As egos, envy and jealousies grew, so did the risks that financiers were willing to take. In the end, many people lost because the intent behind the risks were devoid of values. The banks that flourished did so as a result of effectual management who never swayed from sound spiritual, financial and banking principles.

If you want your money to grow and to benefit many people, deposit it in a financial institution that feels prosperous, looks prosperous and is prosperous. Go in and meet the personnel, see the environment they work in, get a copy of the financial statement and review it with your financial advisor. Find out who is on the board of directors and make a judgment as to whether or not you trust them with your money. Deposit your money in an environment that you believe is the most prosperous. Some financial institutions just ooze with prosperity. You can see and feel it everywhere; in the people, in the surroundings and in their customers. That is where you want your money to be.

𝒲ISDOM FOR TODAY:

Date_____

I find the most prosperous environment for my money and energy and I deposit it there. Where there is prosperity, more will surely come.

𝒮CRIPTURE REFERENCE:

"The plans of the diligent lead surely to advantage, but everyone who is hasty comes surely to poverty." *Proverbs 21:5.*

𝒯HOUGHTS: _____

_____

_____

_____

_____

_____

_____

_____

𝒜CTIONS: _____

_____

_____

I am fearless™

$\mathcal{A}$FFIRMATION:

I have clearly defined financial goals.

$\mathcal{N}$ARRATION:

In order to "hit our goals" we must know what they are. Many people I talk with tell me they want to make $1,000,000. That is a great number. Then I ask them, "How are you going to do it?" Most people then give me a look of dismay and respond, "I don't know how I am going to do it, but I am going to do it." The first steps to all achievement are first, to have a clear and definite purpose in life. I have continually referred to this as following the divine plan for your life. Secondly, you must have clearly defined goals. This is a way to stake your claim to your riches. Third, your goals must be in writing, must be as specific as possible and should have a target date by which you intend to accomplish them. Finally, you must be flexible. Many times the results we are seeking come by slightly changing course while staying focused on the end result.

Also keep in mind that your mind always seeks specificity and clarity. If you want to earn $1,000,000 this year, *you must have a clear path to follow AND you must have a clear mental and written picture of what you are going to do with the money when you receive it.* If you are lacking either of these elements, most likely you will fail in the accomplishment of your goal, or it may take much more time, energy and emotion to accomplish it. If you establish clearly defined goals with a certain road map to follow and a sure picture of what you will do with your riches, then most likely you will have them. I have a detailed description of how to write goals in my book, *Affirmations Of Wealth*, as well as some sample written goals. If you are a novice at goal setting, I recommend that you read *Affirmations Of Wealth*, or any of the other suggested readings in the Appendix to this book.

Writing your goals down gives you clarity, a clear picture of the end result you are seeking, establishes a road map for you to follow, holds you accountable to accomplishing the goal and provides motivation for you if the going gets tough. Write down your goals, visualize the end result and the specific use of the money you will receive. Affirm your belief in the accomplishment of your goals every day. Soon, they will be yours.

WISDOM FOR TODAY:

I Am willing to be held accountable to my goals. I see them clearly because I have put them into writing. Now I take action and the results I seek begin to seek me.

SCRIPTURE REFERENCE:

"Write the vision, and make it plain upon the tablets; that he may run that readeth it." *Habakkuk 2:2.*

THOUGHTS: _____

_____

_____

_____

_____

_____

_____

_____

ACTIONS: _____

_____

_____

I am fearless ™

$\mathscr{A}$FFIRMATION:

I earn, invest, circulate and create money wisely and consciously.

$\mathscr{N}$ARRATION:

The spiritual economy recognizes both the spiritual laws and the money laws. Here are a few of the basic money laws that must be adhered to (remember, money is energy and money is God in action):

You must have a budget. This is particularly important for those of us who spend money unconsciously. Establishing a budget serves many important roles. First, it helps you establish clear earning and spending goals. Second, adhering to a budget mandates that you *stop and think before spending money* and develops the habit of using money consciously. Third, having a budget allows you to see where you may be "wasting" money right now. Remember we must respect money in order to have and keep it. If we continually "waste" money we continually disrespect money. As a result we continually lose or repel money. *You must develop a money consciousness; that is being totally aware of how much money you have, why you have it, where it is, and what you are doing with it.* The more unconscious your are with money, the more likely you will be poor of mind, poor of heart and poor financially.

You must circulate money with love and gratitude. This means you must spend money consciously, spend it for the right reasons, and pass on your love, gratitude and blessings for abundance when you disburse it. This also holds true for gifting or donating money and time. If you gift or donate money or time with an expectation of something in return, you will get nothing in return. If you donate for the tax deduction only, you'll probably get audited. Donate out of love, joy and for the pure happiness of helping someone in need.

You must earn and create money doing something you love or by investing in principle (values) centered investments. The more you love what you do, the more love, happiness and gratitude you create; therefore, the more abundance and wealth you create. When you give your money (energy) to someone else or something else as an investment, invest in the principles and values of the company in addition to the financial soundness of the company.

WISDOM FOR TODAY:

Date_____

I create a fair, honest and realistic budget today. This allows me to circulate and invest money consciously. The more conscious I Am of money, the more money I shall have.

SCRIPTURE REFERENCE:

"Awake my soul, Awake!" *Psalm 57:8.*

THOUGHTS: _____

_____

_____

_____

_____

_____

_____

_____

ACTIONS: _____

_____

_____

I am fearless™

*A*FFIRMATION:

I reduce my current expenses and I invest the difference.

*N*ARRATION:

Most of us could live as well as we are right now or better, spending 10% less than we are spending right now. I can hear your thoughts, " I'm already on a tight budget. My expenses are increasing faster than my income." There are a myriad of creative ways to reduce your expenses and have fun doing so while living better. When was the last time you really analyzed your expenses? List every expense you have and ask yourself, "Is this necessary?" Or ask, "Is there a creative way I could accomplish this while spending less money?" You will be amazed at what you will see and hear.

Many of our expenses are unnecessary, ego gratifying indemnities which allow us to be irresponsible. Reducing your expenses reduces anxiety, worry, real and psychic debt, and increases your consciousness, respect for money and respect for yourself. Now don't get me wrong, you deserve to have everything, you deserve to be wealthy, you can and will be financially free, but only after you build self-respect and respect for money. That is when the money really starts to flow in. ***Respect, love and glorify money as if it were God in action... because it is.*** Then you shall have your fruitful returns.

Of course, when you reduce your expenses, you take the difference and invest it. I have referred to the proper methods of how and where to invest many times already. Follow these guidelines, and your fortune will manifest rather quickly. If you saved 10% of your income for 10 years at even a modest interest rate, you would have more than an entire year's income set aside, even after taxes.

*W*ISDOM FOR TODAY:

Date_____

Today I review all my expenses and I "let go" of what I don't need.
After rationally reducing my expenses I invest the difference. I Am
financially free.

*S*CRIPTURE REFERENCE:

"A man's pride shall bring him low: but honor shall uphold the humble in spirit."
Roman's 8:28.

*T*HOUGHTS: _____

_____

_____

_____

_____

_____

_____

_____

*A*CTIONS: _____

_____

_____

_____

I am fearless™

AFFIRMATION:

I pay taxes fairly and honestly for the God of all concerned.

NARRATION:

In a recent survey in USA Today, approximately 60% of American taxpayers thought it was okay to "slightly" cheat on their taxes. Here is a crucial piece of advice. ***Stop cheating on your taxes, you are only cheating yourself.*** Keep in mind, your subconscious knows what you are doing. The word "cheat" means to swindle, defraud or betray. If you cheat at anything, including paying your taxes, your subconscious starts playing a mental tape, over and over and over, until you remedy the situation. Here is what the tape says, "You are a phony. You are a scoundrel. You are deceitful. You are going to get caught." Sooner or later, you start to believe it. And, when you believe something, you continually carry it out in all aspects of your life. If you are deceitful in paying your taxes, you will always repel money, you will have no respect for money, no respect for the Source of money and no respect for the good it can do for you and for others.

Forget about those worn out excuses. I have heard them all, "The politicians are just going to waste it. I refuse to pay taxes because it will go to a cause I don't support. The government doesn't need it. It's just going to pay for welfare for people who are cheating the government." ***Even Jesus paid taxes. "Render unto Caesar what is his."***

When you pay taxes you are contributing to the common good of many people. Let God take care of the rest. If someone is illegally receiving welfare, pity them. They are poor of mind, poor of heart, poor spiritually and poor financially. The more they cheat, the more they dig a hole of disrespect for God and themselves. These people can never be rich spiritually or financially. Pray for these people. Then pay your taxes.

*W*ISDOM FOR TODAY:

Date_____

I pay taxes out of self-respect and respect for God. God's plan is the perfect plan. When I pay taxes fairly and honestly, I contribute to the common God.

*S*CRIPTURE REFERENCE:

"Render therefore unto Caesar the things that are Caesar's; and unto God the things that are God's." *Matthew 6:33.*

*T*HOUGHTS: _____

_____

_____

_____

_____

_____

_____

_____

*A*CTIONS: _____

_____

_____

I am fearless™

$\mathcal{A}$FFIRMATION:

I now accept the ever increasing riches that are faithfully and continu-ously flowing into my life.

$\mathcal{N}$ARRATION:

All right. Money is now beginning to flow into your life. ***Accept It.*** Once your money begins to flow in, you may experience some feelings of guilt, uncertainty or confusion. "Now that it is coming in, what I am going to do with it?" "The money might change me, change my life." Exactly...congratulations...you made it. Since you have clearly defined goals, a sense of purpose and you know exactly what you are going to do with your new wealth, this isn't a problem for you. Your dreams are coming true!

Some of the old "lack tapes" may start playing in your head. If you start to rationalize and hear things like, "If I make more money, I Am going to have to pay more taxes?" Or, "If I make more money, people may treat me differently." These are only natural self-doubts and fears that you will overcome the more comfortable you get with money and with your new found confidence. Don't shut off the flow. You may struggle with this for a while. Those old thoughts have been working on and in you for a long time. Have the courage and the faith to accept God, accept the money, accept the changes for the better in your life and live your dreams.

It may take several months before your new found confidence displaces your old lack thoughts and scarcity mentality. This is only natural. *Keep in mind, you are not losing a part of yourself, you are gaining the self-respect, love, faith, success and wealth that was always yours by right. Once the flow of money begins, nurture it, love it, perpetuate it and continue to accept it. You deserve it! This is the natural way.*

*W*ISDOM FOR TODAY:

Date_____

I have the courage to live my dreams. I Am fearless in letting money come into my life. I let money continually stream into my life. I let God continually stream into my life.

*S*CRIPTURE REFERENCE:

"For steadfast love is before my eyes, and I walk in faithfulness to you."
Psalm 26:3.

*T*HOUGHTS: _____

_____

_____

_____

_____

_____

_____

_____

*A*CTIONS: _____

_____

_____

_____

I am fearless™

*A*FFIRMATION:

I Am aware of all forms of exchange. I stop and think before I act.

*N*ARRATION:

So you are on the Internet and you are coaxed into trying something for free. Those banners just keep flashing across your screen and you can't resist at least taking a look. **When you buy something, you are actually investing in the product or service you are purchasing, as well as the company and people that produce or render the product or service.** Would you invest in something without doing some research first? Without finding out the facts?

Credit (debt) cards, debit cards, checks, e-commerce, electronic banking, Internet purchasing and investing, and paying bills electronically, are all ways the vendors and financial institutions have told us to make our lives easier and simpler. These things also make us unconscious of money. These systems, while necessary some of the time, "have taken the money out of our hands and out of our minds." Since we no longer handle money, we no longer *think* about it. And if we don't think about money, we have no money. Whenever possible, use actual cash to make your purchases. Handle cash as much as possible. Before writing checks, using your credit and debit cards, or purchasing something electronically, visualize the cash in your hands and being released from your hands. This is a powerful way to *stay conscious of what you are spending.* Never release energy in any of these forms without seeing and feeling it first. This will help you reduce impulse purchases and investing in products and services that you don't really need or want.

There is an old saying, *" cash is king."* Convert every non-cash transaction into a currency transaction in your mind. Stay conscious of money. Stay conscious of what and where you are investing. Only put your energy into circulation at the right time, for the right reason, in the right way and in the right place.

WISDOM FOR TODAY:

Date_____

*I realize that **cash is king**. I Am always conscious of how, why, where, when, for what and to whom I release money. I make good judgments. I invest my money wisely.*

SCRIPTURE REFERENCE:

"Awake thou that sleepest." *Ephesians 5:14.*

THOUGHTS: _____

_____

_____

_____

_____

_____

_____

_____

ACTIONS: _____

_____

_____

I am fearless™

$\mathcal{A}$FFIRMATION:

I Am grateful for the financial success of other people.

$\mathcal{N}$ARRATION:

Truly spiritual minds, minds where there is the most gold to dig, are possessed by people who think win-win. In other words, although wealthy people may be competitive, they also never wish ill-will or harm upon anyone or anything else. *Truly rich people don't focus on "beating" their competitors, they focus on bettering themselves. In our truly abundant universe, there is no need or truth in scarcity thinking.*

Ego is a wonderful terrible thing. A seed that bears two vines. One good and one evil.

John Steinbeck

If we truly are "spiritual beings undergoing a human experience,"* there is no need for false ego, driving us to try to control or conquer other people. To strike gold in the spiritual economy, you must genuinely want other people to succeed and prosper. You must wish them all good things and trust in God's plan. You can only control what God will allow you to control anyway. Everything is working in accordance with His perfect plan. A good piece of advice in this area comes from the Alcoholics Anonymous creed which states: God, grant me the serenity to accept the things I cannot change; the courage to change the things I can; and the wisdom to know the difference.

Have the wisdom to wish prosperity for all people. Have the courage to wish for all people to become fearless and faithful in their actions. And have the courage to accept God's blessings when they are bestowed upon you or upon others.

*Deepak Chopra

WISDOM FOR TODAY:

Date _____

I Am truly abundant in my thinking and in my actions. I wish prosperity upon all people and have the courage to bring to me my own.

SCRIPTURE REFERENCE:

"Do nothing from selfish or empty conceit, but with humility of mind let each of you regard one another as more important than himself." *Phillipians 2:3.*

THOUGHTS: _____

_____

_____

_____

_____

_____

_____

_____

ACTIONS: _____

_____

_____

I am fearless™

AFFIRMATION:

I Am self-disciplined in my money thoughts and in my money actions.

NARRATION:

Sometimes, having more money and creating more money is simply a matter of self-discipline. Most people have a misconception of the true meaning of the word "discipline." Discipline, in its truest sense, means to "cultivate" and to "practice." Carrying the definition one step further, we find the word cultivate is described as "enlighten, reclaim or enrich." The word practice is described as "habit and exercise."

When we are self-disciplined with money, we habitually exercise our enlightenment and enrich ourselves. We reclaim and conserve energy, and therefore, we are able to cultivate it for future growth and enhancement. If you have a gut reaction to the word "discipline" as being something negative or difficult, it will be difficult for you to develop money (or any other type) discipline. Dig a little deeper and picture "self-discipline" as an enlightenment process which always is fruitful. There is no "denial" in self-discipline; there is abundance and enrichment. Forget the old paradigms and thoughts about self-discipline. The "no pain, no gain" mentality is worn-out and useless.

When you exercise self-discipline in your thoughts, in your actions and in your use of money, you produce more, create more, have more. The money is always there for you to enjoy, to circulate and to invest. Begin a process of self-discipline today. Use your money to enrich and enlighten your life.

WISDOM FOR TODAY:

Date_____

I Am self-disciplined in my thoughts and actions. When I Am self-disciplined, I enrich and enlighten my life.

SCRIPTURE REFERENCE:

"Be ye doers of the word, and not the hearers only, deceiving your own self." *James 1:22.*

THOUGHTS: _____

_____

_____

_____

_____

_____

_____

ACTIONS: _____

_____

_____

I am fearless™

AFFIRMATION:

God has invested in me and I Am invested in Him.

NARRATION:

The spiritual economy is created individually and collectively. God has created us as a perfect image of His love. He has given each of us unique gifts and enough talents to created hundreds of fortunes. We are his seeds of abundance. We are how He sows and reaps. *Although we are only one person, we have the power of many. We have the ability to change lives, create abundance, prosperity and wealth. We have love to give and strength to use. We have it all.*

Now we must use it all. As more of us become conscious of the spiritual economy, we will change the world for generations to come. Remember that each thought and action you take creates results forever. Help God. Be a seed of abundance for you, your family, your community, your world. Carry forth His message through your courage, your fearlessness, your love and your money. Your individual spiritual economy can create jobs, instill love and self-respect, invest in projects and people to further God's plan; it can feed the poor and energize the weary.

Post this poem somewhere where you can see it daily. Read it often. It will make a significant difference in your life and in the lives of others.

> I Am only one, but I Am one.
>
> I can't do everything, but I can do something.
>
> What I can do, I ought to do.
>
> And what I ought to do,
>
> By the grace of God, I will do.
>
> Canon Farrar

WISDOM FOR TODAY:

Date_____

I Am an individual dynamo in God's economy. He has invested in me and I will return great dividends.

SCRIPTURE REFERENCE:

"And we know that all things work together for good to them that love God, to them who are called according to his purpose." *Romans 8:28.*

THOUGHTS: _____

_____

_____

_____

_____

_____

_____

_____

ACTIONS: _____

_____

_____

_____

I am fearless™

*A*FFIRMATION:

I Am a gracious giver and receiver.

*N*ARRATION:

I keep the channels of wealth and prosperity open by being a gracious giver as well as receiver of God's abundance. When we are gracious, we are benevolent, compassionate, charitable, unselfish and merciful. We can all understand the feeling of joy and compassion we have when we give a gift. Can you feel just as joyous when receiving a gift? I used to have terrible habit of denying gifts. This was both selfish and unmerciful.

When someone offers you a gift with a true intention, it is your obligation to receive that gift. So many of us have been taught that it is unworthy to take gifts or accept the kindness of other people. Gifts, money, kindness and love are God's love and energy in motion. You must believe you are worthy of God's love. *When receiving gifts we also bless the giver. If we keep denying the flow of abundance that is intended for us, we will close all channels of abundance. It is as important to receive as it is to give.*

It is simple. If we wish to receive wealth into our lives, we must first create a space for the wealth to come. We can do this by giving a portion of our income, our time, our love and our energy to a charity or someone in need. Money isn't the only source of charity. Do you need all the clothes in your closet when there are others that can use them? Do you need to spend every evening (hopefully you spend very few) glued to the television when the need for volunteers is so great in our communities? There is always something you can give, especially love and time.

Keep the channels of abundance always open. Give with love and you shall always have love. Receive with love and you shall always give love.

WISDOM FOR TODAY:

Date_____

I Am charitable both when I receive and I give. I Am joyous to receive and I keep the channels of wealth open.

SCRIPTURE REFERENCE:

"Give and it will be given to you; good measure, pressed down, shaken together, running over, they will pour into your lap. For whatever measure you deal out to others, it will be dealt to you in return." *Luke 6:38.*

THOUGHTS: _____

_____

_____

_____

_____

_____

_____

_____

ACTIONS: _____

_____

_____

I am fearless™

*A*FFIRMATION:

I Am ever restoring my soul with laughter.

*N*ARRATION:

What does this have to do with money and wealth? In order for any of us to truly be prosperous and financially affluent, we must be totally wealthy. That means we must enjoy abundance spiritually, in our families and relationships, financially, mentally, physically and socially. Money is a serious issue. So is success, wealth and many of our other desires. Sometimes we become so focused on wealth and the manifestation of our material desires that we leave a piece of our soul behind.

Laughter allows us to restore our soul, just as a good walk or silent prayer and meditation do. Being able to laugh at ourselves, and the seeming ever present peculiar moments in life, is healthy, wealthy and wise. Who said the world has to be a serious place all the time? God isn't serious all the time. If I can't find people to laugh with or things to laugh at, I laugh at myself. I look back at all the laughable things I have done, or the good times I have enjoyed, and I laugh.

When we laugh, we relieve stress, create a positive frame of mind and replenish our souls. Laughter is also an ally when faced with an adversity or challenge. With God on your side, how could you worry? Plan to achieve your goals and live your dreams, but laugh along the way. Appreciate your accomplishments and celebrate with good cheer.

When you do, you nourish your mind and your soul.

*W*ISDOM FOR TODAY:

Date_____

I Am full of hopes, dreams and laughter today. Laughter restores my soul.

*S*CRIPTURE REFERENCE:

"I saw the Lord always before me...therefore my heart was glad, and my tongue rejoiced." *Acts 2:25,26.*

*T*HOUGHTS: _____

_____

_____

_____

_____

_____

_____

_____

*A*CTIONS: _____

_____

_____

_____

I am fearless™

ᴀFFIRMATION:

I surrender to God and allow His will to guide me to my good.

ᴀRRATION:

This affirmation is a great clarification of the concepts of prayer, trust, faith, intuition, acceptance and synchronization or surrender. **What do we need to pray for? Courage, vision, guidance and the revelation of God's perfect plan for us. In Whom must we trust? God. In what must we trust? God's perfect plan for us. In who must we have faith? Ourselves. What must we accept? The Will of God. What must we surrender? Our ego, our fears, our lack thoughts, our doubts, our perceived limitations. What shall we receive? His guidance and love toward our perfect plan.**

I practiced law for 13 years. I was good at it and earned over six figures a year income. I was in it for the money, the ego, the recognition and the power. I eventually began to hate what I was doing because it was not congruent with who I was as a person. I was in the legal profession for all the wrong reasons. I prayed. I put my trust in God. I demonstrated my faith through actions. I gladly surrendered to His will. I sold my law practice.

I prayed some more and I listened for the answers. I became who I was intended to be; a writer, an author, a motivational speaker and coach, a network marketing entrepreneur. The money came. My wealth came. My physical and mental health came. My happiness came. Love re-emerged. I created and accepted the manifestation of my dreams and contributed greatly to the spiritual economy. I asked. I listened. I acted faithfully and with love. I received. And so shall you.

WISDOM FOR TODAY:

Date_____

I don't need to do it my way. I need to do it His way. Tonight I will sleep deeply, knowing that God will guide me tomorrow to the wealth that I would never have if I had "done it myself."

SCRIPTURE REFERENCE:

"Trust in the Lord, with all your heart. Never rely on what you think you know. Remember the Lord in everything you do and He will show you the way." *Proverbs 3:5,6.*

THOUGHTS: _____

_____

_____

_____

_____

_____

_____

_____

ACTIONS: _____

_____

I am fearless ™

AFFIRMATION:

I live my dreams NOW!

NARRATION:

There is no procrastination in the spiritual economy. There is only here and now. One of the key spiritual laws is the law of acceptance. We each must accept our dreams and desires today, not tomorrow. We must act faithfully today, not tomorrow. When we get the inclination to *wait until later* to do something, a red flag should go up in our heads. We need to ask ourselves, " Why do I want to wait until tomorrow to do this?" Is it a lack of faith, a deep seated fear, indifference or just laziness that is getting in our way.

The truth reveals that unless your intuition is strongly telling you to wait until another time to do something, you should do it now. There are no idle hunches in the spiritual economy, only His guidance. Each day we allow procrastination to get in our way, we lessen the likelihood that we will ever take action on our goals or manifest our desires.

The word "now" also acknowledges our willingness to have something now even if we cannot yet see it. Faith mandates that we believe in what we cannot see, and visualization is the mechanism which allows us to embrace our dreams and have them now. The more we exercise the concepts of now and visualization, the more likely it is that our dreams and goals will manifest. Act, think and accept in the now.

*W*ISDOM FOR TODAY:

Date_____

There is no tomorrow in divine mind, only here and now. I accept the good of the spiritual economy today, and my good soon-after manifests.

*S*CRIPTURE REFERENCE:

"Take therefore no thought for the morrow: for the morrow shall take thought for the things of itself..." *Matthew 6:34.*

*T*HOUGHTS: _____

_____

_____

_____

_____

_____

_____

_____

*A*CTIONS: _____

_____

_____

I am fearless™

*A*FFIRMATION:

*I **Now** attract wealthy and capable people who want to do business with me.*

*N*ARRATION:

This affirmation combines the law of attraction (I attract) with the law of acceptance (now). What and whom do you want to attract to yourself? *If there is one thing that every great spiritual leader, every great business person and every great coach can agree on, it is this; no one can develop wealth, attract money or succeed alone.* There are no "lone wolves" in the spiritual economy. All wealth is developed through people. Where do you think money comes from? Does it just fall from the sky? Of course not. There always has to be en effort of at least two people, usually many more, for wealth to be developed.

This affirmation magnetizes you to attract wealthy and capable people. If you want wealth and money, where else would you look? People who are wealthy already understand the money laws. They already know how the process works. They are spiritually, financially, physically, mentally and socially healthy. You want to both learn from, and do business with, them. Also, the word capable is an adjective. When we use the word capable, we are attracting people who are both intelligent and action oriented.

Finally, quite obviously, you want to "do business." You want to attract and create relationships that will benefit both of you personally as well as financially. Many business relationships, especially the ones you will develop using this process, are also spiritual, social, mentally rewarding and invigorating.

WISDOM FOR TODAY:

Date_____

I am a magnet for wealthy, prosperous and competent people. Together we create an ever increasing stream of financial and personal wealth.

SCRIPTURE REFERENCE:

"Behold, how good and how pleasant it is for the brethren to dwell together in unity." *Psalm 133:1.*

THOUGHTS: _____

_____

_____

_____

_____

_____

_____

_____

ACTIONS: _____

_____

_____

I am fearless™

*A*FFIRMATION:

People are happy to pay me. There is always enough.

*N*ARRATION:

It is especially important to take money from people we know when it is offered. If you render a service to a friend, and they offer you money or some other form of payment, take it graciously and with gratitude. If we get into the habit of "not taking" money from friends, that same mentality carries over into our other relationships as well. If you have a difficult time accepting money from a friend or relative for a service rendered, you will also have difficulty accepting payment from clients. After all, many of your clients are "strangers." If you can't take money from a friend, you surely couldn't take money from a stranger. As a child, you were probably taught not to take things from strangers. Well, money is a thing.

If a friend or relative offers you payment, remember that you are in the spiritual economy. Your friend or relative lives in a world of constant supply. Your love and acceptance mandates this is so. In the spiritual economy, when money goes out, immediately money comes in.

Also, when we don't accept money from people that we know, we build up an emotional and mental bank account. This leads to many broken friendships and relationships. If you helped a friend mow their lawn today and they don't pay you, you may (and this is human nature...it happens almost every time) expect them to do you a favor in return. If you ask a favor of them and they refuse or can't do it, you will be disappointed, hurt and maybe even angry. Remember that cash is king. Use money to pay friends and relatives. It feeds the spiritual economy and opens the channels for more financial success.

WISDOM FOR TODAY:

Date_____

When people offer me money, I accept it with joy. This keeps me in the habit of acceptance and expands the spiritual economy for all to benefit.

SCRIPTURE REFERENCE:

"Be kind to one another." *Ephesians 4:32.*

THOUGHTS: _____

_____

_____

_____

_____

_____

_____

_____

ACTIONS: _____

_____

_____

I am fearless™

*A*FFIRMATION:

I pay myself fabulous dividends through the faithful use of my subconscious mind.

*N*ARRATION:

Do you have the courage to be faithful to God and to yourself? It does take courage to "be different," to not be "part of the crowd." Sometimes people hear the word "subconscious" and they start to think things like, "Am I being brainwashed?" Many people instinctively don't want to change the way they think (if they think at all), because they know it will force them to change. Since there is comfort in mediocrity, many people would rather stay average than risk a small amount of discomfort for the greatness they truly can attain. As a matter of fact, in most cases, we already have greatness within us, we just need to have the courage to expose it.

Our subconscious minds contain vast reservoirs of greatness, wealth and treasures. We can unlock the door to our greatness and step through into the Promised Land, by using the power of our minds. *We are each, literally, a walking gold mine. Our subconscious mind is our gold mind. It knows where the treasure is and how to get there. It contains the universe's most advanced navigation system and it has a direct link to the omnipotent power, God.*

Begin today, to tap into this power. Exercise your subconscious mind. Give it commands. Reveal to it your dreams, desires and expectations. Constantly "talk to yourself" and to God. Carry on a running conversation of wealth, love, abundance and prosperity. The answers are always revealed, *ALWAYS.* Use your *gold mind* instead of your old mind. If you continue to do what you have always done, you will continue to get what you have always gotten. If you continue to think the way you think now, you will continue to get the same results. Clear the channels for your wealth. Release your worn-out thoughts and your negative thinking. Pray, affirm, visualize and act with faith. You will then begin to mine the gold from your ever abundant, ever faithful, *gold mind.*

WISDOM FOR TODAY:

Date_____

All my dreams, desires and treasures are within me now. I manifest my greatness and mine my gold through my own thoughts. I pay myself marvelous dividends.

SCRIPTURE REFERENCE:

"Thanks be to God for His incredible gift!" *2 Corinthians 9:15.*

THOUGHTS: _____

_____

_____

_____

_____

_____

_____

_____

ACTIONS: _____

_____

_____

I am fearless™

*A*FFIRMATION:

I Am free from mistakes and the consequences of mistakes.

*N*ARRATION:

There are no mistakes in divine mind; there are no mistakes in God's perfect plan. There are paths to follow and trails to explore. There is wisdom to gain and lessons to learn. There is faith to exercise and strength to gain. There is love to receive and love to give. But, there are no mistakes.

We are each on a journey of acceptance through faith and trust in God. The only time we really go astray is when our "human minds", our human tendencies, and our inability to surrender to God's will and divine plan for our life takes precedence in our lives. We are all human. We all go astray. To err is a natural process of straightening our crooked paths.

If you are holding on to something "wrong" from your past, let it go. It is over. If you are afraid to venture out because you might "make a mistake." So what. *The only mistake you can make is not having faith in God; not striking out on your divine path, not undertaking your divine adventure.* God has an investment in you and you have an obligation to pay dividends, for His sake and for yours.

So the next time you hesitate because of past "mistakes," or the possibility of future "failure," forget about it. There is no failure in divine mind; there is no failure in God; there is no failure in you.

*W*ISDOM FOR TODAY:

I Am human but I Am divinely human. My perceptions of past mistakes and failures are only that; perceptions. My path has been made straight, my success is assured.

*S*CRIPTURE REFERENCE:

"Come now, let us reason together," saith the Lord: "though your sins be as scarlet, they shall be as white as snow; though they be red like crimson, they shall be as wool." *Isaiah 1:18.*

*T*HOUGHTS: _____

_____

_____

_____

_____

_____

_____

_____

*A*CTIONS: _____

_____

_____

I am fearless™

AFFIRMATION:

I have all the perfect answers...I have a perfect vision...I have a perfect plan...I take perfect actions...I accept perfect abundance, NOW.

NARRATION:

I cannot overemphasize the point that we all have what we seek within our possession, *NOW.* I have spoken and counseled with so many people who tell me they are "in search of" or "seeking" the truth in their lives. They go from class to class, seminar to seminar, guru to guru, *seeking the answers they already have within themselves.* Of course I believe in education and obtaining wisdom and knowledge whenever possible, but please do not overlook the obvious. The answers aren't out there. *The source of your strength and treasure is not out there. It sits in waiting within you.*

At some point in time, we each must acknowledge the truth. When we acknowledge and accept the truth that God is our source, that God is within us and all around us, that we are a perfect expression of His love, that we are deserving of His love, that we must be God in action; then the searching is over and the manifesting begins. Now many of us will continue to search and search even though we know the truth. We may not want to accept our obligation to succeed or accept the goodness that is ours. But those of us who accept the truth, then set out to deliver the truth through our actions; we are the ones who glorify Him while harvesting our bounty.

Please accept the truth. Don't deny yourself. Don't deny God's glory. Don't deny the answers, the people, the love, the money, the perfect ideas or the wondrous expressions of abundance that are yours. You have them now. Look in the mirror. Look yourself straight in the eyes. Be aware of what you see. Listen to what you hear. Pray on these things. Act on these things. Your truth is in there.

WISDOM FOR TODAY:

Date_____

My search is over. I have found the truth. I have always had it within my grasp. Now I set out to manifest my glory in His name and in mine.

SCRIPTURE REFERENCE:

"But seek first his kingdom and his righteousness, and all these things shall be yours as well." *Matthew 6:33.*

THOUGHTS: _____

_____

_____

_____

_____

_____

_____

_____

ACTIONS: _____

_____

_____

I am fearless™

AFFIRMATION:

I always find the simple way to get things done.

NARRATION:

I recently saw an advertisement which only had one word printed on it; *Simplify.* What a great suggestion. The word "simple," in its purest sense, means clear, uncomplicated and essential. Many of us are doubters, critics and outright cynics. Somehow we develop a justification for these attitudes by claiming we are only seeking the truth or we need to "get to the bottom" of something. Keep being a doubter, a critic or a cynic and you will get to the bottom of something...the bottom of the ocean of despair.

There is power in simplicity. There is a purity and greatness in simplicity. Now just because something is simple, doesn't mean it is going to be "easy." But the more we complicate things, for sure, the more difficult we make them. You don't have to attempt to justify your existence by making something more complicated or difficult than it really is. Do all things the simple way. Here is a good example. In the Olympics there are marathon runners and there are steeple chase runners. The marathon runner can run the same distance as a steeple chase runner in half the time with one-third the effort. They are both forms of running but one is a rhythmic, flowing effort toward a goal. In the other, there are real and imaginary obstacles always in the path to the finish line. Your life does not have to be a steeple chase. You don't need imaginary or real obstacles on your pathway. You don't need to create confusion for the sake of justification. This only diverts attention, energy and strength from the truth and from the divine plan of your life.

Make things simple, pure and do what is essential. Clarity, combined with a sense of purpose are the path to all achievement and financial wealth. Do it now...keep it simple.

WISDOM FOR TODAY:

Date_____

I Am simplicity in motion. I Am clear, rhythmic and flowing in all my thoughts and in all my actions. There is no room and no need in my life for complications.

SCRIPTURE REFERENCE:

"Restore me to health and make me live!" *Isaiah 38:16.*

THOUGHTS: _____

_____

_____

_____

_____

_____

_____

ACTIONS: _____

_____

_____

I am fearless™

AFFIRMATION:

I Am a unique expression of God. I have a divine mission to fulfill.

NARRATION:

Some of you may remember the song, *What's It All About Alfie*. This is what its all about; you have a divine mission to fulfill. You already have the unique gifts and talents, or the ability to obtain those unique gifts and talents, within you. You can, if you want to, start using your gifts right now. You can begin to truly be a channel of God's greatness, love and wealth, right now. All you have to do is accept the truth, let go of the worn out and vain conditions that you created in your life, and move into the divine nature of who you are.

I specifically used the words, "and move into the divine nature of *"who you are,"* because we can only have what we want to have in life, and keep it, if we are true to who we are. We can do, be and have all things by being who and what we must be to carry out God's intended purpose. Here is the amazing thing. Think about what you love to do. Think about what you love being. This is, almost without fail, God's intention for you. *Forget about the old "religious" absurdities such as you must "suffer" for God. You have no obligation to "suffer." You have an obligation to rejoice and glorify, to uplift and exemplify, to love and be truthful.*

Be who you want to be, be who you must be, be what you know is the truth for you. This is the way to your amazing good fortune.

WISDOM FOR TODAY:

Date_____

I have the strength to be truthful to my true calling. I don't need to sacrifice, I need to glorify. Today is a day of glorification. Today I live my truth.

SCRIPTURE REFERENCE:

"Before I (God) formed thee in the belly, I knew thee; and before thou camest forth out of the womb I sanctified thee, and I ordained thee..." *Jeremiah 1:5.*

THOUGHTS: _____

_____

_____

_____

_____

_____

_____

_____

ACTIONS: _____

_____

_____

I am fearless™

AFFIRMATION:

I accept the truth and humble myself to its glory.

NARRATION:

I have mentioned many times that one of the keys to manifesting our desires is acceptance. We must accept God, accept ourselves and accept the truth in order to be, do or have the abundance we deserve. The truth is difficult to accept at times. We pray to God and hear an answer that we know is truthful, yet we don't want to accept it. God's direction to us is full of love and perfect for the fulfillment of our divine destiny. Our rejection of His direction is foolish and contrived by ego and our own vain thoughts.

When God speaks, listen. Your subconscious mind is the tool God uses to deliver His messages to you. Your intuitive messages and "hunches" just may be the answer to your prayers. Don't discard anything that God sends to you. Humble yourself and put away your own vain thoughts for a moment. With God there can be no ego, only "we go." With God as your partner, how could you fail?

Surrendering to God's will means surrendering to love, faith, abundance and prosperity. It means truly preparing yourself for the bounty which you are about to receive. It means you will be a channel for God and His divines. It is in the truth which lies within that you will find your riches.

*W*ISDOM FOR TODAY:

Date_____

*I Am truthful with myself by accepting God today. When I accept God,
I clear the channels for my total abundance.*

*S*CRIPTURE REFERENCE:

"...serve him with a perfect heart and with a willing mind: for the lord searcheth all
the hearts, and understandeth all the imaginations of the thoughts." *1 Chronicles 28:9.*

*T*HOUGHTS: _____

_____

_____

_____

_____

_____

_____

*A*CTIONS: _____

_____

_____

I am fearless™

AFFIRMATION:

I Am a reflection of money and money is a reflection of me.

NARRATION:

Money flows in and out of our lives as a mirror of our thoughts about ourselves and about money. There are times when our net-worth is a measure of our self-worth. When we are happy, trusting, loving, and pure of heart, thought and intention, money tends to flow to us. When we are "depressed," envious, jealous or laced with greed, money is repelled by us.

I've had many people say to me, "I have a great self-image and I am an agent of God. I am full of love and good intention, but I have no money." The reason is your paradigm or beliefs are that to be "Godly," or to do the "right thing," you don't need money. You believe truly spiritual people don't need money. After all, Jesus exclaimed that a camel would fit through the eye of a needle before a rich man would enter the kingdom of heaven. Jesus was talking about people who are rich with arrogance, deceit and self-aggrandizement. He was exclaiming the sin of greed and the unworthiness of people who have gained riches through taking advantage of other people. This is not you. Jesus could materialize anything he wanted in the twinkling of an eye, and he did. He had true faith, true riches and true belief in the abundant life.

Then there are those who say, "I must give away my services for free because I am called to do charity." Or, " I must give my services cheaply so more can afford them." Examine your motives when this happens to you. Are you really being charitable or are you simply "cheapening" yourself to gain acceptance?

You must change your beliefs about money. Anything you can do without money, can be done as well, or better, with money. As revealed by Jim Rohn, "Money makes you more of what you already are." If you are full of scarcity, lack and limitation, with your money, you will create more scarcity, lack and limitation. If you are rich in spirit, love, and true intentions, you will be more so the more money you have.

*W*ISDOM FOR TODAY:

Date_____

Today, I release my old negative and limiting beliefs about money.
I can do more with money than I can without.

*S*CRIPTURE REFERENCE:

"For unto everyone that hath shall be given, and he shall have abundance:
but from him that hath not shall be taken away even that which he hath."
Matthew 25:29.

*T*HOUGHTS: _____

_____

_____

_____

_____

_____

_____

_____

*A*CTIONS: _____

_____

_____

_____

I am fearless™

Affirmation:

What I profess I eventually possess.

Narration:

Some religions require their congregations to "profess their faith." The word profess means to "affirm," "assert through declaration," or "lay claim to." What a powerful truth. You can profess a thing and it will be done. Can this be true? The answer is yes. As a matter of fact, the answer is always yes. If you are persistent in your profession, and back your profession with faith (action), it shall always come to pass.

Along with the concept of profession, we must also understand the concept of patience. Patience is the ability to maintain our inner-strength with composure. Patience is having the courage to maintain your faith while God's plan unfolds. God's timing is always perfect; He is never late, never early. We only get into trouble when we want to control the timing of God's intention for us or when we procrastinate out of fear. When you feel yourself "struggling" or "pushing hard" for a solution to a problem, stop. Turn the problem over to God. Ask for His direction. Pray for the answer and it will surely come. Then take action.

When we begin to force an answer to our problems rather than allowing God to deliver the perfect solution, we work against the natural flow of life. Work with God, not against Him. He will let you know when the time is right. Combine God's timing, with your faithful actions, and riches will surely follow.

*W*ISDOM FOR TODAY:

I Am patient when patience is needed. Patience is an act of faith through which I can manifest my riches according to God's perfect plan.

*S*CRIPTURE REFERENCE:

"For the vision is yet for an appointed time...Though it tarries, wait for it; because it will surely come." *Habakkuk 2:3.*

*T*HOUGHTS: _____

_____

_____

_____

_____

_____

_____

_____

*A*CTIONS: _____

_____

_____

I am fearless™

AFFIRMATION:

I Am alive with abundance...prosperity is natural to me.

NARRATION:

The word "alive" suggests vitality and exuberance. When we are alive, we are alert, lively and vital. Is this how you feel most of the time, or are you just surviving? To be abundant, to attract the things you desire in life, you must be full of energy. This is the natural way.

There are millions of people, all around the world, who have been taught or forced to survive. When we are in a "survival" mindset, we are existing, but we certainly are not alive. The survival mentality has been born and bread from fear, lack and mental slavery. All anyone has to do, to shed the shackles of the survival mentality, is exercise the one and only thing over which God has given us complete control; our minds. Attitude surely is everything. Our attitudes dictate who and what we have in life, and why we have (or don't have) them. Our attitudes determine whether we are rich or poor, happy or sad, healthy or sick.

Make up your mind to be alive with abundance. To live an abundant life between your ears. Here is where all prosperity, wealth and riches are located. Here is where they are stored, waiting for you to claim them. God has already delivered them to you and has given you the tool (your mind) by which you may manifest them. Exercise your mind and every form of wealth can and will be yours.

WISDOM FOR TODAY:

Date_____

I exercise my mind by living today. I seek out the positive energy in all things and I let the rest go. When I Am alive, I truly live.

SCRIPTURE REFERENCE:

"And whatever ye do, do it heartily, as to the Lord, and not unto men."
Colossians 3:23.

THOUGHTS: _____

_____

_____

_____

_____

_____

_____

ACTIONS: _____

_____

_____

_____

I am fearless™

*A*FFIRMATION:

I accept all the goodness money can bring to me.

*N*ARRATION:

For the last time, money is good and is a form of goodness. Money can only be "bad" and the "love of money" can only be the root of evil, if you allow it to be so. Remember that money is simply a medium of exchange. It is either paper, precious metals or other material items that represent value. The actual value lies in your thoughts, beliefs and actions. Money is exchanged and flows to you according to what you believe and are willing to accept.

If you are truly willing to prepare yourself for and accept riches, you shall have them. You must prepare spiritually, mentally and financially for the wealth you desire, and you must be prepared for the responsibility that comes with wealth. Are you willing to invest your wealth wisely? Do you know what you will do with your wealth when you receive it? Are your prepared to circulate your wealth freely, with gratitude and love, by investing some, spending some and gifting some of it away? Are you prepared to carry out God's plan for you and for your wealth? Are you willing to enjoy and immerse yourself in prosperity? These are the questions you must be able to answer now, in order for your wealth to materialize.

When you think of money, think of God. When you think of money, think of goodness. When you think of money, think of love, kindness and generosity. When you think of money, think of happiness, greatness and abundant joy. Associate yourself with the goodness money can bring, and the money will surely come.

WISDOM FOR TODAY:

Date_____

I associate money with all good things. I can receive, create and give greatness through my thoughts and through my money.

SCRIPTURE REFERENCE:

"Come. O blessed of my Father, inherit the kingdom prepared for you from the foundation of the world." *Matthew 25:34.*

THOUGHTS: _____

_____

_____

_____

_____

_____

_____

ACTIONS: _____

_____

_____

_____

I am fearless™

*A*FFIRMATION:

I reclaim my power over money.

*N*ARRATION:

Many of us get into financial trouble because we have given up our spiritual and mental energy to someone else or to something else. ***Money is a form of energy that we can easily lose control to if we allow this to happen.*** Here is an example. Steve decides he "needs" new floor mats for his car. He doesn't have the cash so he charges it to his credit (debt) card. The floor mats cost $500 and they look great in his car. After a few months, the floor mats get a little worn and they are beginning to fade. Steve has only paid the minimum payment on his credit card, which barely covers the interest payment. This goes on for months and Steve begins to resent the fact that he is still paying for something he bought a year ago and no longer has the same appeal to him. Steve is upset and in order to make him "feel" better, Steve goes out and buys a new stereo, and, you guessed it, charges it to his credit (debt) card. Now he is still paying for the floor mats he doesn't "need" any more and a new stereo. Things are starting to escalate. This cycle continues until Steve can no longer charge anything else to his credit cards and he starts to worry about how he is going to pay for all of this "stuff." You see Steve has lost his individual power to the power of 5th Avenue, and to the power of the credit card company. They now have control over him and he is going to pay for it dearly. At 17% interest, Steve will actually pay 2 or 3 times the amount of the purchase price of the items he bought and he now has to go out and make more money, or deprive himself of some essentials in life to pay for his powerless thoughts.

If this scenario sounds familiar to you, make the decision today to cut all your credit cards in half and toss them in the trash. The physical act of cutting the cards and discarding them is a very important subconscious message which proves you are now serious about taking control over your money thoughts and are willing to become responsible with your money. Establish a budget for paying off your credit (debt) cards by paying 10% more than the minimum payment, even if this is only a small amount. You will "pay off" your balances far in advance than you would have if you didn't do this and you will save hundreds, if not thousands, of dollars in non-tax deductible interest payments. More importantly, you will begin to reclaim control over your credit cards, your flow of money, and your self-respect.

WISDOM FOR TODAY:

Date_____

I Am in control of my money; my money doesn't control me. I Am responsible and conscious of where I allow my energy and power flow. I stop and think before I spend or invest money.

SCRIPTURE REFERENCE:

"Stand at the crossroads and look; ask for the ancient paths, ask where the good way is, and walk in it, and you will find rest for your souls..." *Jeremiah 6:16.*

THOUGHTS: _____

_____

_____

_____

_____

_____

_____

_____

ACTIONS: _____

_____

_____

I am fearless™

$\mathcal{A}$FFIRMATION:

I liberate myself from past negative money experiences. I Am free to become wealthy.

$\mathcal{N}$ARRATION:

What an extraordinarily important affirmation! Many of us attend seminars, read books and listen to tapes about changing our lives and becoming more successful. We get motivated and inspired and off we go. We begin to make changes and we see a glimmer of hope that we are finally "going to be successful." We are finally going to have the things in life we want to have and do what we want to do, then BANG, we hit an obstacle. That obstacle is our stored memories of past negative money experiences. It jumps up like a goblin and snatches away our dreams. *You see, you can go to all the "success" seminars in the world, you can read all the books and listen to all the tapes, and it won't do any good unless you are comfortable and enthusiastic about making, creating and accepting money.* If you have continual money difficulties, there is a solution to your problem.

Go to a quiet place where you can be alone. Close your eyes, relax and clear your mind of any anxieties or worries. Sit in silence for a few minutes and then ask yourself, "What is (are) the negative money memory(s) that are holding me back from achieving financial freedom?" For all of us who have or have had financial difficulties, there is always a corresponding negative money memory that is stored in our subconscious. This memory continues to hold us back forever, unless we address it, accept it and eliminate it. For me, it was a feeling of guilt about money. Our family was poor. Being raised by a single mother on welfare, I always felt guilty when my mother tried to buy me something or give me money because I new she couldn't afford it, or so I thought. I continually rejected money and developed the habit of doing so well into my 30's. When I did accumulate money, I would always find a way to lose it because I felt guilty about having it. And even to this day, I have to make a conscious effort to accept and accumulate wealth. As a result of feeling guilty about receiving welfare, I also continually found ways to stay "indebted" to the government. I had consistent tax troubles for several years.

I have many other restrictive money memories that crippled me for years, until I discovered what they were, why I had them, forgave myself and others for them, and then cleared the channels (through prayer, affirmation, visualization and faithful actions) for my financial success. You can do this as well. Allow your past negative money memories to come to the surface in your mind. Analyze your past and current financial situations and see how your past negative memories about money have hindered your financial success. Be truthful about these things. Write them down and make up your mind to eliminate them. Use the process in this book to free yourself forever.

*W*ISDOM FOR TODAY:

Date_____

I Am free at last from my past negative experiences with money. What happened in the past is gone and I now clear the channels for my financial success.

*S*CRIPTURE REFERENCE:

"The discretion of a man deferreth his anger; and it is his glory to pass over a transgression." *Proverbs 19:11.*

*T*HOUGHTS: _____

_____

_____

_____

_____

_____

_____

*A*CTIONS: _____

_____

_____

_____

I am fearless™

*A*FFIRMATION:

I Am responsible for the financial future of my family. I teach my children well.

*N*ARRATION:

The thoughts, paradigms and attitudes we pass on to our children about money are just as vital as the genetic make-up and heritage we pass on to them. If we had a genetic abnormality which was unique to our family, we would do everything we could to protect our children, and help them overcome the challenges they may face in life as a result of this problem. Well, we do the same thing with our thoughts and attitudes about money. Look at your financial situation right now, especially your thoughts and attitudes about money; then stop and think about how close they are to those of your parents. This can almost be frightening. We portray to the financial make-up of our parents almost with the same certainty that we portray the genetic make-up of our parents.

But today is the day of your amazing good fortune. A truth has been revealed to you that may never have been revealed to them. You can and will take control of your financial life and the future financial freedom of your family. *By changing your thoughts about money, and taking control of your attitudes and actions with money, you can change the financial future of your family for generations.* You have the God given charge and a personal responsibility to do this. Think of the money heritage you have already passed on to your children. How do they feel about money? What do they do with it when they have it? Can they enjoy money and use it responsibly? If you don't like the answers to these questions, look within yourself and ask "How did I pass on this money heritage to my children?"

Begin to teach your children the spiritual laws about money. Talk positively about money and people who have it. Show them the goodness they can create through their rich thoughts and actions. Teach them how to live with money, not how to survive without it. Play money games with your children. Have them do a little research and buy them a few shares of stock. Let them make the financial decisions about their stock. Make up a sample stock or mutual fund portfolio and let them trade it or manage it. You can do this on the computer on any online service for free. Teach your children the spiritual and financial goodness they deserve and the wondrous things they can accomplish in life with this goodness. Your family's financial heritage begins today.

*W*ISDOM FOR TODAY:

Date_____

I Am in control of my family's financial heritage. I teach my children about the goodness of money and the spiritual and financial rewards life has to offer.

*S*CRIPTURE REFERENCE:

"Train up a child in the way he should go, even when he is old he will not depart from it." *Proverbs 22:6.*

*T*HOUGHTS: _____

_____

_____

_____

_____

_____

_____

_____

*A*CTIONS: _____

_____

_____

I am fearless™

AFFIRMATION:

I Am respectful of myself...I Am respectful of money.

NARRATION:

There is a money law which always holds true. If you respect money, money will respect you. Money always responds to people who respect it. If you spend money wastefully, without respect for the result of your spending, you will repel money forever. If you spend money consciously, with good intention, with respect for yourself and for the good your money is providing, you will continually attract money.

Although your self-worth should not be a reflection of your net worth, your net worth can certainly be a true reflection of your self-worth. Most people who are irresponsible in one area of their lives are usually irresponsible in many, if not all, the areas of their lives. So, self-respect is an important energy that our money recognizes and images. Your money will follow the pattern of self-respect you create. If you are the type of person who is always late for an appointment, you will always be late when financial opportunity arrives for you. If you are the type of person who always seems to find problems, you will continually find money problems. If you are not physically fit, you may not be fiscally fit. Our attitudes about ourselves are typically our attitudes about money. If we are overweight physically and mentally, we are probably overweight (in debt) financially. If we do not attend church or lack a spiritual foundation, we probably lack a financial foundation.

The bottom line is this: If you want to have more money and keep it in your life, you must have more respect for yourself. Gain control of your self-respect and you can gain control of your entire life. God is on your side; money can be on your side as well, if you respect it.

WISDOM FOR TODAY:

I Am respectful and fit in all areas of my life. As I build my self-worth, I open the channels to build my net worth.

SCRIPTURE REFERENCE:

"...be an example (pattern) for the believers, in speech, in conduct, in love, in faith, and in purity. *1 Timothy 4:12.*

THOUGHTS: _____

_____

_____

_____

_____

_____

_____

ACTIONS: _____

_____

_____

_____

I am fearless™

*A*FFIRMATION:

I only spend what I see.

*N*ARRATION:

Here is a clear-cut money law. Invest more, spend less. Many of us get caught up in the "its only a few dollars" syndrome and then end up nickel and dimeing ourselves into financial bondage as a result. Now be aware, I am not talking about being cheap here. I am not trying to limit you to an overly strict budget. But many people lose consciousness about money, and as a result, it filters out in subtle ways that can devastate us in the long run. If you are employed by someone else and you have a 401k, 403b (or something similar) plan, contribute the maximum allowed by law to these plans. The difference over many years of employment between contributing the minimum and the maximum amount can be hundreds of thousands of dollars.

"But I need every penny that I bring home," you say. For the next week, write down every penny that you spend. Everything! Then take a look at what you spent and why you spent it. If you are like most people, you will be shocked at where your money goes. You will quickly discover you can easily make the additional contribution to your 401k or IRA that you haven't been making and build yourself a tremendous financial future.

I urge you to continually think wealthy thoughts. You must create and live in a wealthy environment, but also be responsible with your money. Add up all the money that you simply throw away through wasted purchases, excess eating and drinking habits, smoking and other destructive habits during the course of your lifetime; this will add up (with interest) to hundreds of thousands of dollars. Have fun, live a wealthy and healthy lifestyle, but do it consciously and responsibly. Don't throw away your money. When you throw away your money, you throw away a piece of yourself, a piece of your financial future, a piece of God.

WISDOM FOR TODAY:

Date_____

I Am rich in consciousness about money. I Am aware of what I spend and what I release. I live a life of wealth through responsibility.

SCRIPTURE REFERENCE:

"Where there is no vision, the people perish..." *Proverbs 29:18.*

THOUGHTS: _____

_____

_____

_____

_____

_____

_____

_____

ACTIONS: _____

_____

_____

_____

_____

I am fearless™

ℐFFIRMATION:

I Am timely with money and money is timely with me.

ℕARRATION:

I cannot over state the importance of recognizing the connection between time and money. In a very real sense, time is money. Also, the time value of your investments can be staggering. If you invest money regularly, over time, it grows and flourishes. The longer period of time, the more your money grows. For example, if you invest $200 per month at 10% interest for 20 years your account balance will be $151,873.77. But if you invest $200 per month at 10% interest for 30 years your account balance will be $452,097.58. WOW! Start investing now! Start investing for your children now!

A great way to do this is to establish IRA accounts for your children when they are very young. A $50 per month contribution to an IRA at 10% interest for 50 years accrues to $866,219.54. Can you imagine? $50 per month for your children starting at age 5 or 10, (they can take over the contribution when they begin to work) and they will be millionaires at age 60, even of they didn't make any other type of investment. Of course, these are simple illustrations. I have not accounted for inflation and other economic factors, but the truth is most of us spend more than $50 per month on coffee in the morning. *You see, financial freedom really is a choice. The use of time as your ally is a choice.*

Make healthy and smart choices about where you spend your money and your time. Invest it wisely, to your advantage. Use time as your ally and you will be enriched in all ways.

*W*ISDOM FOR TODAY:

I understand the relationship between time and money. The better I invest them, the more I have. I invest my money wisely over time and then I Am enriched with both.

*S*CRIPTURE REFERENCE:

"Walk in wisdom...redeeming time." *Colossians 4:5.*

*T*HOUGHTS: _____

_____

_____

_____

_____

_____

_____

_____

*A*CTIONS: _____

_____

_____

I am fearless™

𝒜FFIRMATION:

I Am truthful in all my financial affairs.

𝒩ARRATION:

All truth begins with God and ourselves. *In order to manifest and create money, we must be truthful. We must be honest about our spiritual relationships, our personal and professional relationships, our relationship with ourselves and our relationship with money. In order to be truthful, we must be honest about where were stand right now, then we can build from there.* To be truthful in our financial affairs, we must be truthful in our personal affairs.

Truth is a habit. The more truthful we are in one area of our lives, the more truthful we will be in all areas of our lives. What do you need to stop doing right now in your life that is untruthful? How will you stop this and when? What do you need to start doing in your life to be more truthful? How will you do this and when?

I urge you to list the 6 areas of your life (see below) and write next to each one the truth about that part of your life right now. Then list how and by when you will change this. Here is a simple format (write as many truths and solutions in each area of your life as possible, then prioritize and schedule them):

Area Of Life/ Priority	My Present Truth/Where I Am Now	Change Required
Spiritual / 1	Need to be closer to God on a regular basis.	Meditate daily for 20 minutes beginning today.
Family / 2	My wife and I don't see each other enough.	Commit to a weekly date night. We will go on a date every week starting this week.
Financial / 3	My credit card debt is out of control.	Call credit card company and ask them to lower my interest rate. Destroy card today!
Physical / 4	I am 20 pounds overweight.	Exercise 3x a week starting this Saturday.
Mental /5	I haven't read a new book in a while.	Buy a new personal development book tomorrow and read it.
Social / 6	I haven't volunteered in a year.	Call my Pastor and review volunteer schedule.

When you complete your inventory, the truth about yourself will be revealed. This can be a little scary but it is necessary in order to create both spiritual and financial wealth. Once this exercise is complete, don't hesitate. Begin to implement your changes immediately. You may not implement them all at once, but at least begin to make the change(s) that is the most important. Your intuition will guide you.

WISDOM FOR TODAY:

Date_____

I Am truthful with God and myself today. I have the courage to be spiritually and financially free through the truth. I do an honest evaluation of my life and I make the changes necessary for my total freedom.

SCRIPTURE REFERENCE:

"The God who made the world and everything in it, being Lord of heaven and earth, does not live in shrines made by man, nor is he served by human hands, as though he needed anything, since he himself give all men life and breath and everything...Yet he is not far from each one of us, for In him we live and move and have our being." *Acts 17:24-28.*

THOUGHTS: _____

_____

_____

_____

_____

_____

_____

_____

ACTIONS: _____

I am fearless™

ᴀFFIRMATION:

I keep good company with my money.

ɴARRATION:

The spiritual economy and the laws of money respect your choices about money. If you make poor choices, the spiritual and financial laws give you poverty. If you make conscious and smart choices, the spiritual and financial laws give you riches. You can train your subconscious and conscious minds to make smart choices by doing the little things right. *Most people think the "little things" are insignificant or aren't worth the time necessary to implement them. But these "little things," and how you handle them, establish a pattern of respect or disrespect for money and for God.* Again, the more you respect money, the more it will respect you.

Here are some "little things" that you can do to establish the habit of respecting your money, thereby attracting more to yourself (add your own recommendations to this list, there are many more):

1. Deposit your money in the highest yielding accounts. "So what," you say. The bank on the corner is only paying .125% more than my bank. Well .125% more is more. You will earn more and prove your respect for money.
2. Refinance your mortgage, if it makes sense to do so, to a lower interest rate.
3. Don't tithe your money, gift it freely. The concept of tithing is greatly misunderstood. Tithing, in its original form as established by Jewish law, was an "obligation to pay" a portion of your income, crops or livestock to the local authority in return for which you would be given a blessing in return. This was similar to a tax. Gifting, or giving your money to a charity you have a sincere interest in, is giving with no obligations or expectations in return. Jesus never proclaimed tithing as a spiritual law or obligation. He proclaimed giving from the heart as an expression of love for those in need.
4. Shop less often. If you are responsible for buying your family groceries for example, make a detailed list of what you are going to purchase and stick to it. Shop once a week instead of twice a week. You will save hundreds of dollars during the year.
5. Call your credit (debt) card companies and ask them to lower your interest rate. You will be surprised at what will happen. If they won't lower your rate, find a company that will charge you a lower rate and transfer your balances.

Date_____

6. Bless your money and when it is in your home, keep it in a sacred place. Establish a place of prosperity for your money and keep it there. When you circulate money, send your blessings with it.

These are only six of the "little things" you can do to enhance your money magnetism. There are many more. Become a student of what happens when you handle, circulate and invest your money properly. Repeat what works and eliminate what doesn't, but always do the little things right.

*W*ISDOM FOR TODAY:

I always do the little things right with money. I Am conscious of what I physically do with money, and why I do it. I respect money and money respects me.

*S*CRIPTURE REFERENCE:

"Many...have done well, but you excel them all." *Proverbs 31:29.*

*T*HOUGHTS: _____

_____

_____

_____

_____

_____

*A*CTIONS: _____

I am fearless™

AFFIRMATION:

I Am a treasury of creative financial ideas.

NARRATION:

The richer we are in our thinking, the richer we become. Our thoughts and ideas really are the treasure-troves of financial freedom. When we become more conscious of our finances, and how the spiritual and money laws interact in our lives, we become very cognizant of money, how to spiritually perpetuate it, and how to be creative with it.

This affirmation specifically uses the word "treasury" because of the true meaning of the word treasury is synonymous with "treasure-house." **The store house of all our treasures is in our spiritual gold minds. Pick up a thesaurus and look at what you find when you research the meaning of these words.**

You will find treasury and treasure-house linked with the terms "God-send," "gold mine," "windfall," and "treasure-trove." Your creative ideas are all of these things and more... if you put them to use. It doesn't matter what your profession or career is, you can substantially increase your income and make more money by being creative (within or outside of your profession). I know many teachers who create more money "part-time" from creative business ideas than they do "full time" as a teacher. I know police officers who earn twice as much money from enterprising ideas then they do from "making a living" as a police officer. The simple truth is you are not restricted to how much money you can earn or create because of a job title. You are only restricted by your thinking. This is very important for those of you who are professionals. I have seen countless CPAs, lawyers, doctors and other professionals stagnate their incomes because they are doing well "in comparison" to other professionals. The rational goes something like this, "The average income for a doctor in my field is $80,000 per year and I am making $110,000 per year, so I am doing well." You may be earning above the average, but there are doctors earning $110,000 per week from their profession as well as other creative business ventures. The moral is, don't limit your income by limiting your vision of what can be done, regardless of your chosen profession or career. Forget about comparing yourself to what others are doing and focus on realizing your potential and fulfilling your God given destiny. Then you will be rich.

WISDOM FOR TODAY:

Date_____

My treasury of creative ideas is a store house of wealth. I tap into the treasury in my mind and I mind the gold which is waiting for me.

SCRIPTURE REFERENCE:

"Do not lay up for yourselves treasures on earth, where moth and rust consume and where thieve break in and steal, but lay up for yourselves treasures in heaven (in your subconscious mind), where neither moth nor rust consumes and where thieves do not break in and steal. For where your treasure is, there will be your heart also." *Matthew 6:19-21.*

THOUGHTS: _____

_____

_____

_____

_____

_____

_____

_____

ACTIONS: _____

_____

I am fearless™

*A*FFIRMATION:

I Am comfortable in the spiritual and financial worlds of money.

*N*ARRATION:

In order to have money and continually attract it, you must be comfortable with it. ***In its truest sense, the word comfortable means, "to be at ease with." When we are comfortable with money, it tends to flow into our lives like water from a tap.*** But most people are not comfortable or at ease with money. For many people, even just physically handling money creates anxiety and fear.

There are many ways to become comfortable with money. The first way is to understand that money is good, purposeful and plays an important role in God's economy. Secondly, you must eliminate any negative thoughts or attitudes you have about money regardless of whether those thoughts were inherited from someone else or were created by you. Third, you must get used to physically handling money in a responsible manner. Don't be afraid to physically hold onto your money. Before you spend money, look at it. Stop for a moment and examine the bill and notice what you see and feel. Fourth, always carry your money "the green side up." All US currency has a "gray" side and a "green" side. On the green side, you will see the words "In God We Trust" printed. On one-dollar bills you will also see the inscriptions "ANNUIT COEPTIS" and "E PLURIBUS UNUM." Translated, these inscriptions mean "God has favored our undertakings," and "One made of many." Pass on your trust In God by physically passing your dollars the green side up. By doing so you perpetuate God's intent for favored undertakings to many. Fifth, always release money with a positive, grateful and loving attitude. Send forth your blessings and well wishes for prosperity when you release it.

Make these five steps for being more comfortable with money habitual. Always stop and think about money before you pass it on.

*W*ISDOM FOR TODAY:

I am comfortable and at ease with money because I understand the goodness it creates. I pass on my trust in God and my blessings to all when I handle money consciously.

*S*CRIPTURE REFERENCE:

"Give and it will be given to you...For by your standard of measure it will be measured to you in return." *Luke 6:38.*

*T*HOUGHTS: _____

_____

_____

_____

_____

_____

_____

_____

*A*CTIONS: _____

_____

_____

I am fearless™

AFFIRMATION:

I Am Fearless tm.

NARRATION:

This affirmation is the first affirmation I ever wrote. ***In Affirmations of Wealth - 101 Secrets of Daily Success, I described fear as nothing more than our own perception of what "might" happen. Most fears are unwarranted and never come to pass.*** The same holds true for our fears about money, wealth and poverty. One of the 9 basic fears is the fear of poverty. And unfortunately, this is why we have so much poverty in the world. Since many of us focus on lack, limitation and poverty through our fears, that is exactly what we mandate.

I Am Fearlesstm is a very important affirmation to use daily, because it applies to all areas of our lives. Of what are you afraid anyway? There are many theories that people don't succeed in life because they are afraid of failure, afraid of success or afraid of change. There may be some limited truth to those theories, but I believe most people don't succeed in life because they simply don't know how. Most people are not fortunate enough to have role models and coaches of success and prosperity in their lives from an early age. The reason most successful people have successful children is because they pass on their mentality about success, money and freedom to their children beginning at a very young age. Successful people take the mystery and fear out of success by making it a natural part of their lives and the lives of their children.

Be fearless in accepting God. Be fearless in heading your household and raising and loving your children. Be fearless in creating, making and increasing wealth, money and prosperity. Be fearless in developing physical and mental health. Be fearless in accepting and delivering social responsibility. Do the right things and do them often. Do them fearlessly, simply because you know they are right.

WISDOM FOR TODAY:

Date_____

I Am Fearless in all that I do. I Am Fearless in creating wealth. When I create wealth I Am working for God and He is working for the good of all.

SCRIPTURE REFERENCE:

"I sought the Lord, and He heard me, and delivered me from all my fears."
Psalm 34:4.

THOUGHTS: _____

_____

_____

_____

_____

_____

_____

ACTIONS: _____

_____

_____

I am fearless™

*A*FFIRMATION:

I Am financially free.

*N*ARRATION:

Regardless of how much money you earn, you can be financially free. Being financially free is a function of your attitude, your intent and your control over money. There a people earning $35,000 per year who are financially free in comparison to people who earn $500,000 per year who will be in debt for the rest of their lives. Being financially free has a direct correlation to your beliefs in God, your beliefs about the goodness of money, the debt you incur and the energy you pass on.

To be financially free, you must believe your are pursuing God's intended mission and purpose for you, and you must accept whatever that may be. You must carry out your mission with love. Next, you must believe money is good and that money can only be "bad" if it is used for a bad purpose or with a bad intention. You must accept goodness in all forms, including money. You must eliminate debt, both financial and emotional. The baggage of past mistakes, prior poor decisions and unconscious thinking (and spending), can weigh us down forever. Free yourself from whatever you must to become financially free. If you must free yourself from a relationship, do so. If you must free yourself from an addiction, do so. If you must free yourself from emotional burdens, do so. Whatever forms of debt you are accumulating or holding on to must be eliminated. The simple act of beginning to reduce your financial or emotional debt can be one of the most freeing experiences of your life. In other words, you must take control of what you can and turn the rest over to God.

When you are free emotionally, you are free to pass on your freedom to others. The longer you remain "burdened" by your past choices and experiences, the more "burden" you will create in your life and the lives of others. Make up your mind to be free in all areas of your life, and financial freedom will follow as naturally as the morning light follows the evening darkness.

WISDOM FOR TODAY:

Date_____

I Am free financially and emotionally. I release all burdens to God and I take control of my debts. When I Am debt free I Am totally free.

SCRIPTURE REFERENCE:

"So the people shouted when the priests blew with the trumpets: and it came to pass, when the people heard the sound of the trumpet, and the people shouted a great shout, that the wall fell down flat, so that the people went up into the city, every man straight before him, and they took the city." *Joshua 6:20.*

THOUGHTS: _____

_____

_____

_____

_____

_____

_____

_____

ACTIONS: _____

_____

I am fearless™

AFFIRMATION:

I know exactly how my money is doing at all times.

NARRATION:

Many people tend to want to "forget about their money." They want to turn their money over to a banker or financial planner and forget about it. This is a major mistake. You have an obligation and responsibility to know what your money is doing at all times. It is your money, your energy, your expression of love, your fruit of well placed labor; why would you completely turn it over to someone else? If you have a tendency to do this, stop! Immediately!

When you completely forget about your money, it will completely forget about you. It will take on someone else's energy. I strongly urge you to use a prosperous financial advisor, but stay involved with your money. Make your own investment decisions with the help of your advisor, but you must have the final say. Have regular meetings in-person with your financial advisor and speak to her often by telephone. Use your intuition and if you get a negative "gut feeling" about something your financial advisor has done, said or recommended, find out why immediately. It is your money.

If you subscribe to an on-line service, build yourself an on-line portfolio. You can "keep sight" of your money and investments at any time. If you see something you don't like, investigate it and change it if necessary. *Your money can be childlike at times. The more you pay attention to it, the more love you give it and the more presence you have with it, the more it will respond in kind to you. Never forget about your money and it will never forget about you.*

WISDOM FOR TODAY:

Date_____

I Am always attuned to my money. I know where it is and what it is doing at all times. I never forget about my money and it never forgets about me.

SCRIPTURE REFERENCE:

"You hold me with your right hand. You give me counsel." *Psalm 73: 23,24.*

THOUGHTS: _____

_____
_____
_____
_____
_____
_____
_____

ACTIONS: _____

_____
_____
_____

I am fearless™

*A*FFIRMATION:

All my financial affairs are in order.

*N*ARRATION:

You are the guard at the watchtower of your family's financial future. This certainly is not a book about investments, insurance, wills or trusts, but I must recommend you undertake some simple financial strategies. You must first find a financial advisor who you are comfortable with and whom you trust. Then, you must review the following items with her.

1. Should I have a will, a living trust or some other type of estate plan?

2. Should I own life insurance. If so, what type and why? Is whole life, universal life or term life the best investment for me and my family? Why? Always ask this question of an independent financial advisor who is not going to sell you the insurance.

3. Should I own disability insurance? Why or why not?

4. Should I purchase long term care insurance? Why or why not?

5. Should I have a durable power of attorney or health care proxy? Why or why not?

6. What is the best investment plan for me and my family? Why?

7. What are the tax implications of my investments and my estate plan?

8. How do you get paid? How much commission are you earning?

Each of these questions can be broken down into greater detail, but this is a good starting point. *It is an absolute must, however, that you employ a financial advisor who is sensitive and appreciative of your desires and your goals. She should be compatible with, knowledgeable of, and open-minded to your spiritual, financial, family, emotional and social concepts of money, and your money background. If your financial advisor does not take a sincere interest in you, your goals, your past experiences with money and your future expectations, find someone else.* Remember, you are responsible for your family's financial future. Ask the right questions. Get all things in order. Good things will happen.

*W*ISDOM FOR TODAY:

Date_____

I have a clear plan for my family's financial future. I have a solid foundation for our growth now and well into the future.

*S*CRIPTURE REFERENCE:

"A wise man will hear and increase in learning, and a man if understanding will acquire wise counsel." *Proverbs 1:5.*

*T*HOUGHTS: _____

_____

_____

_____

_____

_____

_____

_____

*A*CTIONS: _____

_____

_____

_____

I am fearless™

Affirmation:

I Am current on all my tax obligations.

Narration:

The payment of taxes is an obligation. You may not like it, but it is a necessity. *Remember the back of your dollar bills and coins, "E PLURIBUS UNUM," one made of many. How could you live the abundant life you are capable of living if you didn't have your country, its infrastructure, its natural resources, its people and its money, readily available to you? That is exactly what you have in most of the free world. You can make all the political, social and economic arguments you want, but the payment, collection and proper distribution of taxes is a necessity for your financial wealth.*

So you don't agree with the government's stance on abortion, the military or social programs. Are you really foolish enough to deprive yourself of the greatness you can attain, and the good you can create, because you don't want to pay taxes? Not paying taxes is one the poorest excuses for neglect I have ever seen. It is outright cowardly. Of course you should have a tax advisor or CPA who properly counsels you on proper tax deductions and the impact of them on your financial affairs, but to neglect paying taxes is a direct assault on your ability to develop wealth.

Pay your taxes. Plan for them properly. Neglect or ignorance is no excuse for the lack of paying your taxes. If you fail to take this step, you will find overwhelming financial and emotional road blocks to your financial success and freedom. The lack of payment of taxes, on time and in the right amounts, can create a blockage to your flow of money and riches unlike any other. So do the right thing. Be honest, be fair. Do the right thing and the right thing will happen to you.

*W*ISDOM FOR TODAY:

I Am current with all my tax obligations. When I Am all square with my taxes, the channels are always open for my financial success.

*S*CRIPTURE REFERENCE:

"Wealth obtained by fraud dwindles, but the one who gathers by labor increases it." *Proverbs 13:11.*

*T*HOUGHTS: _____

_____

_____

_____

_____

_____

_____

_____

*A*CTIONS: _____

_____

_____

_____

I am fearless™

Affirmation:

I Am intuitive about money.

Narration:

Intuitiveness is a natural and innate faculty we each possess. Our intuition can guide us to the treasure within, or keep us out of harms way. It is amazing, but our intuition is always right. Just think back on all the times you have thought, "I should have listened to myself." Our intuition is like a compass, it always points true north. Many hikers and explorers have gotten into trouble because, although they had a compass, they denied its directions. The same holds true for pilots who ignore their instruments and fly by the seats of their pants. This inevitably leads to trouble.

Our inner compasses have been fine tuned by years of experience. It is a mix of spiritual guidance, experience, instinct and ethical seasoning. When we use our intuition, we trust in God, and combine our skill, wisdom, maturity, judgment and practice to make decisions which are, most typically, best for us. The same intuition should be combined with research and sound investment principles to make good decisions about money.

Here is a personal example. About 9 weeks ago, I decided to invest some of my IRA money in stock. I watched the Financial News Network and noticed that all the Internet stocks had been soaring. However, most of these stocks had been soaring on pure speculation, not on sound financial criteria such as earnings, track record in the industry or future growth and earnings expectations. So I asked myself, what companies meet this criteria in the Internet industry and why should I invest my energy in this company? I found one company, Cisco Systems, that was profitable, had a sound plan for future growth and seemed to be a valued centered company. I purchased the stock at $60 per share. It closed this week at $92 per share (as of the date of this publication it had doubled and split). I combined intuition (my gut instinct that the Internet industry would continue to grow) with knowledge (the research I did on the company). I am familiar with the Internet industry, and I understand how that particular industry works. This was a sound financial decision, using my intuition, trust and research. This is always a winning combination.

*W*ISDOM FOR TODAY:

Date _____

*I Am intuitive about money decisions. I combine wisdom, experience
and research to make better decisions and bring marvelous returns.*

*S*CRIPTURE REFERENCE:

"The wise have eyes in their head, but fools walk in darkness..." *Ecclesiastes 2:14.*

*T*HOUGHTS: _____

_____

_____

_____

_____

_____

_____

_____

*A*CTIONS: _____

_____

_____

_____

_____

I am fearless™

*A*FFIRMATION:

I give money generously and respectfully...My heart is an open channel of love and compassion.

*N*ARRATION:

Do you feel as if your financial channels are blocked right now? Are you doing the right things but money isn't flowing in yet? Give some money to a worthy charity and you will open the door for abundance. Be careful here. This is not a bartering system which you can employ to get on God's good side. You can't give with expectations of anything in return. However, when you give for the pure joy of giving, for the love of what you can do to help a fellow person in true need, then your channels open.

Unlike many other experts in this field, I don't believe you must take a certain percentage of your income and gift it away. *What is much more effective is the regular giving of a meaningful gift to a charity, person in need or organization that needs your love and compassion.* I see so many people getting caught in the trap of giving money to an organization simply because they were pressured into it by a business associate to gain a business advantage, or because they want the tax deduction. What a waste of time, energy and money. *The organizations you give to need your love as much as they need your money. They need your compassion, your respect for their people, their work and their efforts. Charitable organizations need your loving and generous mentality to produce results continuously for God's sake, for their sake and for yours.*

Put the same time, effort, energy and love into the charities you donate to as you do with your investments. In a very real sense, your charitable giving is one of the greatest investments you can make. Give freely, generously, lovingly and wisely. Your gifts will multiply many times over.

WISDOM FOR TODAY:

Date_____

When I give to charity, I give lovingly and compassionately. My only expectations are that my love will find the right home and do God's work for the good of all concerned.

SCRIPTURE REFERENCE:

"Love never fails, never fades out or becomes obsolete or comes to an end."
1 Corinthians 13:8a.

THOUGHTS: _____

_____

_____

_____

_____

_____

_____

_____

ACTIONS: _____

_____

_____

I am fearless™

AFFIRMATION:

I Am a person of value under God.

NARRATION:

What a powerful affirmation. I wish I could take credit for it but this affirmation was given to me by Ms. Norma Hale of Austin, Texas. Of all the affirmations I have ever used, I would have to say, "I Am Fearless tm" and "I Am a person of value under God," are the two most meaningful for me. This affirmation confirms every principle I have set out in this book. The words, " I Am," are confirming our God-like being, our spiritual presence and our rich birthright. The word, "person," exclaims we are someone. We deserve "to be" and "we are" of God's heritage. The word, "value," denotes our significance, our worth and our eminence. When we are of value, we have purpose and meaning in our lives. And the term, "under God," certainly indicates that we are God's servants; that we must each surrender to His will to gain true wealth, prosperity and abundance. We are on His mission, for His purpose, for His glory.

This affirmation is the essence of this philosophy; to be rich, we must be rich in spirit, in love, in heart and in our minds. We are worth far more than money. Money is simply one of the tools we use to help create, proliferate and pass on our spirit, our love, our hearts and our minds.

You are valuable in all respects. You are loved by God in all respects. You are worthy of all good things. You have been given the gifts you need to glorify Him and manifest your destiny as well as your financial wealth. Believe in your value, create value and share your value. This is also God in action.

WISDOM FOR TODAY:

Date_____

God creates everything from love. I Am of value to Him and He is of value to me. Together we glorify Him.

SCRIPTURE REFERENCE:

"Herein is love, not that we loved God, but that he loved us, and sent his Son to be the propitiation for our sins. Beloved, if God so loved us, we ought to love one another." *1 John 4:10,11.*

THOUGHTS: _____

_____

_____

_____

_____

_____

_____

_____

ACTIONS: _____

_____

_____

I am fearless™

Affirmation:

I Am selfless in my success.

Narration:

God has made His investment in me. I have reaped great rewards. It is now my duty to share my success for His benefit. The abundance mentality is a mentality of sharing, giving, sowing and reaping. My success, the success of this book, the financial rewards it will generate, are due to my willingness to hear His word, to do His work, to share His wisdom. How can I take the credit when I have just been the channel of His love?

A few years ago, a book was written entitled, *Conversations With God,* by Neale Donald Walsh. There was an outcry by many people in the formal religions, especially the Christian community, because Mr. Walsh claims to have had a continuous conversation with God for several years. The fundamentalists have proclaimed this is impossible...God has proclaimed He will not reveal Himself to any man again until the Second Coming through Jesus Christ.

God reveals Himself to each one of us every day. I am not very familiar with Mr. Walsh's book, but I do know *evidence of God's presence is all around us. The next time your child tells you they love you, look in their eyes and you shall see God. The next time you listen to Mozart or Vivaldi, you shall hear God. The next time you pray and carry on a conversation with God, you shall feel God. The truth is, for us to lead a rich life, we must be continually talking with and listening to God. We must hear His guidance, sense His presence, receive and give His love, use His gifts and answer His calling. This is the answer to your prayers.* God is here and He lives within you.

WISDOM FOR TODAY:

Date_____

*I realize my actions, when they are true, are an extension of God.
I live in His glory as the channel to do His will.*

SCRIPTURE REFERENCE:

"Then you shall see and be radiant." *Isaiah 60:5.*

THOUGHTS: _____

_____

_____

_____

_____

_____

_____

_____

ACTIONS: _____

_____

_____

_____

I am fearless™

*A*FFIRMATION:

I Am disciplined and detailed in all my financial dealings.

*N*ARRATION:

Most people don't realize that discipline is a positive energy, a positive force in our lives. Most people associate pain or denial with discipline. Nothing could be further from the truth. Simply put, discipline means restraining ourselves in the face of temptation. We are tempted in many ways each day. Should I spend money on this item that I don't really need? Should I use my free hour to exercise or watch television? Should I help my daughter with her homework or spend an hour surfing the Net?

In a very true sense, we make choices on a cost benefit analysis all the time. A problem arises when we can't immediately see the costs of our poor choices. Spending an hour surfing the Net instead of helping your daughter with homework may not seem to have an immediate cost, but it has a long lasting effect in many ways. Buying something you don't need (or maybe even you don't want) creates a chain of negativity, guilt, lack and limitation. Not exercising for a week, may lead to an attitude of indifference which ultimately carries a high price.

And so it is with money. Are you disciplined enough to have it in great abundance, or will you manifest only what your prior actions and thoughts dictate you can handle? You can have everything you want financially or materially and still be disciplined. As a matter of fact, discipline is a prerequisite for establishing a healthy and respectful relationship with money. Discipline is a virtue which God has revealed as truth many times. Become more disciplined in your financial affairs and your wealth with begin to flow.

WISDOM FOR TODAY:

Date_____

I see discipline as a positive means to develop wealth. I create a flow of abundance through my disciplined application of all the money laws.

SCRIPTURE REFERENCE:

"Do you see a man skilled in his work? He will serve before kings; he will not serve before obscure men." *Proverbs 22:29.*

THOUGHTS: _____

_____
_____
_____
_____
_____
_____
_____

ACTIONS: _____

_____
_____

I am fearless™

𝒜FFIRMATION:

I Am all, I have all. The divine will of God has manifested into completeness.

It is done. It is so. You are whole. You are complete.

SCRIPTURE REFERENCE:

Date _____

"His Lord saith unto him, 'Well done, thou good and faithful servant: thou hast been faithful over a few things, I will make thee ruler over many things'..."
Matthew 25:21.

THOUGHTS: _____

_____

_____

_____

_____

_____

_____

_____

ACTIONS: _____

_____

_____

_____

I am fearless™

RECOMMENDED READING SELECTIONS

ℛECOMMENDED READING SELECTIONS

As A Man Thinketh by James Allen.
New York: Grosset & Dunlap, 1992.

Ageless Body, Timeless Mind by Deepak Chopra.
New York: Harmony Books, 1993.

First Things First by Stephen Covey, A. Roger Merrill, & Rebecca R. Merrill.
New York: Simon & Schuster, 1994.

Creating True Prosperity by Shakti Gawain. Novato, CA: New World Library, 1997.

The Corporate Mystic: A Guidebook For Visionaries With Their Feet On The Ground by Gay Hendricks & Kate Ludeman. New York: Bantam Books, 1996.

Think And Grow Rich by Napoleon Hill.
New York: Hawthorne Books, 1966.

Wherever You Go There You Are: Mindfulness Meditation In Every Day Life by Jon Kabat-Zinn. New York: Hyperion, 1994.

The Spiritual Lives of Great Composers by Patrick Kavanaugh.
Nashville, TN: Sparrow Press, 1992.

JESUS, CEO: Using Ancient Wisdom for Visionary Leadership by Laurie Beth Jones. New York: Hyperion, 1995.

The Power of Your Subconscious Mind by Dr. Joseph Murphy.
Englewood Cliffs, NJ: Prentice-Hall, 1963

The Dynamic Laws of Prosperity by Catherine Ponder.
Englewood Cliffs, NJ: Prentice-Hall 1962.

EMPOWERMENT: You Can Do, Be, And Have All Things! By John Randolph
Price. Carlsbad, CA: Hay House, Inc., 1996.

The Wisdom Of Florence Scovel Shinn by Florence Scovel Shinn. New York:
Simon & Shuster, 1989.

The Debt-Free & Prosperous Living Basic Course by John Cummuta.
Debt-Free & Prosperous Living, Inc. 310 Second Street, Boscobel, WI 53805
1-888-570-6010 (On Audio-Cassette Only)

CONTACTING THE AUTHOR & PRODUCT ORDERING INFORMATION

CONTACTING THE AUTHOR & PRODUCT ORDERING INFORMATION

About The Author

V. John Alexandrov is a top money earner in the network marketing industry and co-owner of Fearless, Incorporated, a motivational seminar, services and products company. John is a well known inspirational and motivational speaker in the direct selling, network marketing, real estate and financial services industries. He is a former attorney and radio talk show host and resides in Worcester, Massachusetts with his wife Eileen and their four children. John is a graduate of Trinity College, Hartford, CT and the New England School of Law, Boston, MA.

The Leadership Skills Of V. John Alexandrov

John Alexandrov facilitates a series of personal and professional development programs which primarily focus on developing the skills and attitudes necessary to succeed as an entrepreneur. These spiritually based programs have been used by thousands of entrepreneurs in the direct selling, network marketing, real estate and financial services industries. Through the implementation of a principle-centered self-discovery, goal-setting and wealth development process, John helps people to achieve their personal and business goals while enriching their spirit and living a well-balanced life. John is also well-known as a personal development coach. He has an extensive list of personal coaching clients, most of whom are entrepreneurs building their businesses through spiritual principles.

For more information, you may contact:

V. John Alexandrov
Fearless, Incorporated
128 Newton Avenue North
Worcester, MA 01609

∾

email: fearless@excelonline.com
www.iamfearless.com

∾

1-508-757-0953 phone
1-508-757-0472 fax
1-888-404-6257 toll free

∾

You may order additional copies of this book by calling
1-508-757-0953 (phone), 1-888-404-6257 (toll free), 1-508-757-0472 (fax)
or shopping at our website at www.iamfearless.com.

We hope you are enjoying *Your Spiritual Gold Mind – The Divine Guide To Financial Freedom.* The following is a list of other products available from John Alexandrov (please call to order):

Affirmations Of Wealth – 101 Secrets Of Daily Success (book – 288 pages)
Price $19.95

Beyond The Goal (audio tape series, approx. 80 minutes)
Price $19.95

Affirmation Greeting Cards (8 inspirational greeting cards per box)
Price $10.00

John is available for speaking engagements. If you would like him to contact you, email John at fearless@excelonline or call him at 508-757-0953. If you would like to be added to John Alexandrov's email distribution and mailing list, please complete the following information & send it (or email it) to the address above:

Your Name: _____

Address: _____

P.O. Box or Mail Stop: _____ ____ _____

City, State, Zip Code: _____

Country: _____

Phone, Fax: _____

Email, Website URL: _____

www.iamfearless.com